Public School Education Foundations

Advancing Opportunity, Excellence, and Innovation

Michael J. Worth

Sanjay K. Pandey

Holly Kamm Wahl

BLOOMSBURY ACADEMIC
NEW YORK • LONDON • OXFORD • NEW DELHI • SYDNEY

BLOOMSBURY ACADEMIC
Bloomsbury Publishing Inc, 1359 Broadway, New York, NY 10018, USA
Bloomsbury Publishing Plc, 50 Bedford Square, London, WC1B 3DP, UK
Bloomsbury Publishing Ireland, 29 Earlsfort Terrace, Dublin 2, D02 AY28, Ireland

BLOOMSBURY, BLOOMSBURY ACADEMIC and the Diana logo are trademarks of Bloomsbury Publishing Plc

First published in the United States of America 2026

A catalog record for this book is available from the Library of Congress

ISBN: HB: 979-8-7651-8850-7
PB: 979-8-7651-8851-4
ePDF: 979-8-2163-5177-1
eBook: 979-8-2163-5176-4

Typeset by Newgen KnowledgeWorks Pvt. Ltd., Chennai, India

For product safety related questions, contact: productsafety@bloomsbury.com.

To find out more about our authors and books, visit www.bloomsbury.com and sign up for our newsletters.

Contents

Acknowledgments

The authors are grateful to the foundation executives who participated in interviews concerning their foundations, listed below. In addition, each reviewed a draft of the case study on their respective foundation and offered corrections wherever necessary. Some also provided suggestions regarding the overall project.

Stephannie Bailey, Chief Executive Officer, Indianapolis Public Schools Foundation

Rebecca Clarkin, Executive Director, Children First Fund: The Chicago Public Schools Foundation

Tim Eby, Executive Director, Special Education Foundation, Special School District of St. Louis County

Kathryn Epps, President and Chief Executive Officer, Fund for the School District of Philadelphia

Rachael Tutwiler Fortune, President, Jacksonville Public Education Fund

Kerry Lynn Franco, President and Chief Deputy of Strategic Partnerships and Innovation, Greater Los Angeles Education Foundation

Sam Gelinas, Vice President of Programs, Strategy, and Development, Greater Los Angeles Education Foundation

Sara Hazel, President and Chief Executive Officer, Denver Public Schools Foundation

Jim Kline, President and Executive Director, DC Public Education Fund

Mike Taylor, Chief Executive Officer, Knox Education Foundation

Michelle Wallis, Executive Director, Austin Ed Fund

The authors express particular appreciation to Mike Taylor, who was chief executive officer of the Knox Education Foundation and chair of the board of the National Association of Education Foundations at the time of this study, and to Jim Kline, president and executive director of the DC Public Education Fund. Both provided advice to the authors regarding the study and assisted them in enlisting the participation of other foundation CEOs.

Introduction

This book includes a collection of case studies on foundations established to raise and manage private funds to support public school systems. These nonprofit organizations are sometimes identified as "local education foundations" (LEFs) (e.g., Abzug et al., 2016), "K-12 Education Foundations" (e.g., Caruthers, 2017), "education foundations" (e.g., Clogston, 2021), or "public school educational foundations" (e.g., Haddad, 2022). This book uses the term "public school education foundations" in order to distinguish these entities from education foundations that support higher education institutions, to clarify that the K-12 schools they support do not include private institutions, and that while they are local rather than national, some do support broader geographic areas, such as counties. Some of the organizations considered in this book are named "foundations," while others use the term "fund."

It is important to clarify that the public school education foundations considered in this book are different from parent-teacher associations (PTAs), parent-teacher organizations (PTOs), booster clubs, and similar organizations. Those types of organizations may indeed be more widely known, but they typically raise funds for an individual school (Nelson & Gazley, 2014). The foundations we consider in this book operate at the school-district or county level, although they may provide grants to support programs in individual schools. Some district-wide education foundations do support charter schools as well as traditional public schools but this book does not discuss fundraising by individual charter schools. The cases discussed in this book do not include community foundations, which in some instances are conduits for gifts to support public schools. They also do not include private foundations (e.g., the Bill & Melinda Gates Foundation) that make grants to support public education, often with the purpose of implementing favored reforms. This book does not include an extensive discussion on the broad topics of school financing or the management of school districts, but rather is focused on public school education foundations and their work.

The opening chapter references some research studies, but the intention of this book is to provide practical insights that may be helpful to those who work with public school education foundations. The case studies look inside the foundations to explore how they are governed, how they raise funds, and how they design and evaluate programs to have an impact. The authors' hope is that the information provided in this book will be of particular interest to foundations' professional staff members, school superintendents, principals, school board members, members of foundation boards, and members of communities who are interested in public education. Chapters including the case studies are numbered simply according to the order in which the studies were completed.

Selection of Foundations and Study Methods

The foundations included in case studies in subsequent chapters were not selected randomly and it is not possible to generalize from these examples to all public school education foundations. A variety of models were represented even among the small number of foundations studied and it was observed that additional variations exist across the country. Again, the authors' intention was to provide selected examples that may inform professionals working in school districts or with affiliated foundations, rather than generate comprehensive data.

The authors began by reviewing a list of the 120 largest school districts in the United States, as identified by the NCES (2022), based on the assumption that large districts would be most likely to have affiliated foundations with comprehensive programs, substantial fundraising operations, and professional staff. The authors searched for foundations affiliated with these largest districts using Google and reviewed the foundation websites to identify those providing robust information on their programs, especially those that appeared to address the goals of advancing opportunity, excellence, and innovation. The authors also reviewed the Form 990s of these foundations. Some foundation executives who participated in interviews early in our project offered suggestions of other foundations that might be of interest and the authors further explored those. Foundations also were selected to achieve geographic diversity across regions of the United States. The authors note that some foundation websites do not facilitate contact, requiring an online form and not including direct email addresses for foundation officers. A few that were of initial interest did not respond to outreach by the authors.

The studies are based on publicly-available materials as well as on interviews with foundation executive officers. The interview protocol was reviewed and approved by the Institutional Review Board of the George Washington University, with which the authors are affiliated. The foundation executives were provided with the interview questions in advance. The interviews were conducted using Zoom and were recorded with the executives' permission. The executives were sent a draft of the case study related to their foundation so that they could note any errors. Any substantive corrections were incorporated in the final drafts.

Overview of Chapters

Chapter 1 provides an overview of relevant literature and some previous research on public school education foundations. It is followed by case studies, each comprising one chapter. A concluding chapter summarizes the authors' observations based on the case studies and offers some conclusions and suggestions for building foundations to advance opportunity, excellence, and innovation in their districts. The authors' backgrounds and some suggestions for further reading are provided at the end of the volume.

References

Abzug, R., Olbrecht, A., Sabrin, M., & DeLeon, E. 2016. Nonprofit financing to the rescue? The slightly twisted case of local education foundations in New Jersey. *Nonprofit and Voluntary Sector Quarterly*, 45 (1), pp. 133–149.

Caruthers, D. 2017. Stepping up: The nation's top K-12 education foundations. Caruthers Institute. Accessed June 22, 2024. https://resources.finalsite.net/images/v1655151060/bhisd/tnoyictmzvlixycvbyot/Caruthers2017Rankings.pdf

Clogston, N. G. 2021. The influence of private contributions in public education: An examination of education foundations. Dissertation, University of Houston-Clear Lake.

Haddad, D. 2022. The importance of public school educational foundations. *NonProfitPRO*. Accessed June 22, 2024. https://www.nonprofitpro.com/post/the-importance-of-public-school-educational-foundations/

NCES (National Center for Education Statistics). 2022. Enrollment, poverty, and federal funds for the 120 largest school districts, by enrollment size in 2021: School year 2019–20 and fiscal year 2022. Accessed November 3, 2024. https://nces.ed.gov/programs/digest/d22/tables/dt22_215.30.asp
Nelson, A. A. & Gazley, B. 2014. The rise of school-supporting nonprofits. *Education Finance and Policy*, (4), pp. 541–566.

1 Providing a Margin

Elementary and secondary education is a major undertaking in the United States. During the 2021–22 school year, there were more than 13,000 public school districts, enrolling more than forty-six million students. There are various types of districts and structure varies across the states. For example, some districts include only elementary schools, some only secondary schools, and some are unified districts that include both. Some are independent districts that function as autonomous governmental units, while others are dependent, functioning as a unit of a town, city, or county government (Ballotpedia, n.d.).

Tax revenue remains by far the largest source of funding for public schools, but growing philanthropic support has gained increasing attention (Ballotpedia, n.d.). Among the most visible sources of philanthropic support for public schools are public school education foundations, which are the focus of this book. This chapter discusses the role of such foundations, adopting the margin-for-excellence perspective that has been long applied to similar foundations in higher education. It then reviews the history and evolution of public school education foundations, their legal structure and requirements, governance, and fundraising. The chapter concludes with findings of research on how to build effective foundations and a review of methods that some have applied to evaluating their effectiveness.

Poised to Provide a Margin for Excellence

If tax revenue remains the largest source of funding for public schools, why are public school education foundations worthy of our interest? The answer may be best understood by looking at the history and evolution of similar foundations that support public universities. In 1961, the National Association of State Universities and Land-Grant Colleges (now the Association of Public and Land-Grant Universities) issued a pathbreaking report, entitled *Margin for Excellence: The Role of Voluntary Support in Public Higher Education*. The report noted that "tax dollars can support basic needs such as the building and maintenance of classrooms, libraries, [and] laboratories, and can provide average salaries for staff members." (National Association of State Universities and Land Grant Colleges, 1961). However, the report argued, achieving a margin for excellence, through competitive faculty salaries, increased student aid, and introduction of new and enriching programs, would require a higher level of private support, that is, philanthropy. The concept of a margin for excellence became the primary justification (case for support) articulated in fundraising on behalf of public colleges and universities in decades that followed.

Most public universities raise and manage philanthropic funds through an institutionally related foundation. Like the public school education foundations, we are considering, these foundations are legally independent of the university, but often are closely related and generally provide support to advance priorities identified by the university administration. The very first such foundation, the KU Endowment, was established in 1891 to support the University of Kansas; but the growth of such organizations came much later in most states. There are today more than 1,400 such foundations, many raising substantial amounts (Council for Advancement and Support of Education, n.d.).

The role of higher education foundations has expanded in recent decades, with significant declines in government support for public universities in some states. Indeed, by 2020, the Association of Governing Boards of Universities and Colleges (AGB) essentially declared the end of the margin-for-excellence era, observing that "today [institutionally-related foundations at public universities and colleges] act more as key philanthropic and entrepreneurial partners that actively support the institution's basic business and operating model" (AGB, 2020).

The margin-for-excellence concept offers a way to understand the impact of public school education foundations. Even foundations that provide relatively modest funding in proportion to overall school budgets or the number of students enrolled may have an impact by focusing on specific groups of students or specific needs of schools. Many also fund innovations that subsequently become adopted on a larger scale. In other words, while not replacing or significantly augmenting tax revenues for general operating purposes, foundations may have an impact by supporting purposes that might otherwise not be undertaken as part of a school district's normal operations. As the Fund for the School District of Philadelphia explains,

"The private donations that we contribute to the District do not supplant government monies. Rather, we introduce new funds to start or sustain cutting-edge, evidence-based models that improve student outcomes" (Fund for the School District of Philadelphia, 2024). It is reasonable to think that like foundations in higher education, public school education foundations may come to play a larger role in supporting public school districts in the future.

Overview of Public School Education Foundations

There is no comprehensive inventory that identifies how many public school education foundations exist. Form 990s filed annually by foundations with the Internal Revenue Service are publicly available; with some researchers having searched the forms to compile data. For example, Ashlyn Aiko Nelson and Beth Gazley identified 16,383 nonprofit organizations supporting public schools by using keyword searches and classification codes developed by the National Center for Charitable Statistics (Nelson & Gazley, 2014). However, the majority of their sample included Parent Teacher Associations (PTAs) and Parent Teacher Organizations (PTOs) rather than the foundations we are discussing. In 2022, Duke Haddad claimed that there were "more than 3,000" public school foundations in the United States, a total that has been widely cited, although Haddad does not explain the method of arriving at that number (Haddad, 2022). Foundations are common, at least in larger school districts. In 2024, the authors searched for foundations affiliated with the 120 largest school districts in the United States and identified 117 such foundations (NCES, 2022). Various articles continue to mention rapid growth in the number of foundations, although specific data is not provided.

Foundations are varied in their service areas. While some support a single school district, others serve a broader geographic area, such as a county that encompasses multiple districts. For example, the Greater Los Angeles Education Foundation partners with the Los Angeles County Office of Education (LACOE) and serves eighty school districts, many of which also have their own foundations. Some foundations support charter schools as well as traditional public schools, but others give only to district programs and traditional public schools, with charter schools raising their own funds. Public school education foundations are to be distinguished from PTAs and PTOs, which generally provide gifts only to specific individual schools, although some foundations also support school-based programs and some maintain online platforms that permit donors to support specific schools.

Activities commonly supported by public school education foundations include professional development for teachers; college-preparation and scholarships for students; early-childhood and pre-school programs; enrichment experiences beyond the classroom, and after-school programs focused on tutoring, training, and other purposes. Some foundations have provided funding for facilities projects, including play spaces and libraries. Others support experimentation with innovative programs having the potential to generate systemic change. For example, the DC Public Education Fund, serving the District of Columbia Public Schools, "connects philanthropy with DCPS' boldest and most cutting-edge ideas … [raising private dollars] to innovate the way kids learn, how and what teachers teach, and what's ultimately possible for an urban public school district" (DC Public Education Fund, 2024). The Fund for New York City Public Schools explains a similar purpose: "The Fund enables philanthropic seed funding to test and accelerate promising ideas within New York City Public Schools (NYCPS), tracks impact and promotes learning, and supports the scaling of solutions that drive excellence in education across NYCPS" (Fund for New York City Public Schools, n.d.). Some foundations also serve as fiscal sponsors, receiving and administering funds for projects or programs offered by organizations that have yet to achieve independent nonprofit status.

Beyond raising philanthropic funds and making grants to support school programs, some foundations play additional roles, including advocating for education funding, engaging communities with schools, and creating ambassadors for public schools (Haddad, 2022). Although most foundations have a close relationship with the district they support, and some have been established at the district's initiative, they are all legally independent. They are governed by a board of directors that is separate from the school board or other authority governing the school system, although some foundation boards do include school officials.

Historical Evolution and Evolving Missions

Some authors date the beginning of public school education foundations in the United States to 1983, when the Ford Foundation provided seed funding for fifty-three foundations across the nation, with the goal of improving public schools in low-income communities (Abzug et al., 2016). Others emphasize the origin of such foundations in California following the passage of Proposition 13 in a ballot referendum in 1979 (Abzug et al., 2016). Proposition 13 limited property taxes, a primary source of support for schools. The result was a significant reduction in funding for schools, with California falling from the fifth highest state for per-student funding to 47th in the nation over the following two decades (Fensterwald, 2022). It also resulted in an equalization of public funding across school districts, to the detriment of wealthier districts. Some of the wealthier districts responded by creating foundations to raise private funds to supplement their public funding and secure their financial advantage. For some observers, continuing such advantages became synonymous with the pursuit of philanthropy to support public schools in the years that followed (Abzug et al. 2016). This understandably raised concerns about the role of philanthropy in perpetuating educational inequity.

However, Rikki Abzug and co-authors (2016) studied foundations on the East Coast and concluded that the intent of the early California foundations to preserve the advantages of wealthy districts was different from what they called the "national model," which included raising private funds to enhance educational resources more broadly. Some continue to express concerns about the influence of private giving on public education and the implications for equity. However, most criticisms focus on gifts directed to individual schools, often through PTAs or PTOs, booster clubs, and similar organizations, which may "enable wealthier parents to essentially buy better education" (Nisbet, 2021). In some states, including California, laws have been enacted to address this concern by restricting the use of funds given to specific schools and requiring that some portion be reallocated to a district-wide education foundation to fund grants based on need. Many districts also have adopted a "centralized fundraising" approach, in other words, a formal relationship between the school district and a foundation that raises and distributes funds to support district-wide initiatives (Nisbet, 2021). However, there continue to be proposals for adopting tax and other policies to assure that philanthropic support of public schools will have the result of reducing rather than enhancing inequity (Nisbet, 2021).

Some urban school districts have identified equity and improved educational quality in traditional public schools as priorities. For example, in describing an expansion of the MPS Foundation, serving the Milwaukee Public Schools, a member of the foundation board explained, "This is all about making sure MPS children get the same opportunities as the most successful choice and charter schools, which all have robust fundraising arms" (Richards, 2016). The foundation's expansion also is described as a strategy for keeping Milwaukee's schools on pace with schools in more affluent suburban districts. MPS's programs include grants to teachers to implement innovative ideas, offering virtual advanced placement courses, and raising funds for an arts program in low-performing Milwaukee schools (Richards, 2016).

Similarly, the San Francisco Education Fund explains, "we are driven by a vision for equity in our schools and in our work with one another" (San Francisco Education Fund, n.d.). The foundation emphasizes its support of "priority schools" within the San Francisco Unified School District, which it defines as "schools that serve the most under-resourced populations." The priority schools have more than 50 percent of students below proficiency in English and math, more than 50 percent students of color, and more than 50 percent of students who are from a "low socio-economic demographic bracket" (San Francisco Education Fund, n.d.). The mission statements and programs of many public school education foundations reflect similar emphases.

Legal Status of Foundations and Implications

Public school education foundations are nonprofit organizations incorporated under state law and classified by the Internal Revenue Service (IRS) under Section 501(c)(3) of the federal tax code. However, there are two broad types of "foundations" covered by Section 501(c)(3) and it is important to understand the distinction. Many of the foundations whose names are most familiar, for example, the Bill & Melinda Gates Foundation, are classified by the IRS as private foundations. Private foundations are funded through gifts from one or a few individuals, often a family, or by a corporation. For example, the Gates Foundation was established with gifts primarily from Bill and Melinda French Gates, and the Walmart Foundation is funded by the Walmart Corporation. While some private foundations do operate their own programs and are known as operating foundations, most make grants to support programs at other nonprofit organizations. Some private foundations have been prominent in supporting public schools, especially to support specific reforms. A well-known example is the role played by the Gates Foundation in promoting adoption of the common core curriculum.

Another category of foundations classified under Section 501(c)(3) includes those classified as public charities. Often described simply as public foundations, these organizations receive gifts from multiple donors and then make grants to support programs at other nonprofit organizations. The public school education foundations considered in this book are public foundations, as are many other foundations established to support public entities, including for example, parks and libraries. Community foundations, some of which do make grants to support public schools, also are public charities that receive gifts from multiple donors and make grants to support organizations serving their communities. The authors searched for foundations associated with the 120 largest school districts in the United States and identified 117. Of that total, 113 were independent public foundations, 3 operated under the umbrella of community foundations, and 1 was a private foundation.

Public and private foundations face different legal requirements. For example, under the law in 2025, a donor who makes a cash gift to a public foundation may claim a federal income tax deduction up to 60 percent of their income while a donor who gives to a private foundation is limited to a tax deduction up to 30 percent of their income. As of 2025, private foundations must spend, on grants or operating expenses, an amount equivalent to 5 percent of the fair market value of their assets in any year. Public foundations do not have such a requirement. Private foundations pay an excise tax on their investment earnings, which public foundations do not. Both types of foundations are required to file an annual report with the IRS. Foundations that are public charities, file Form 990, while private foundations file a variation, Form 990-PF.

The IRS considers classification as a private foundation to be the default for a nonprofit organization and those that are able to qualify as public charities generally are careful to meet the requirements of that status, including what is known as the public support test, in order to avoid the requirements placed on private foundations.

Increasing Professionalization of Public School Education Foundations

The management of public school education foundations has become increasingly professionalized, following a pattern observed in universities and many nonprofit organizations. The growing importance of fundraising and philanthropy in higher education and the nonprofit sector over the past several decades has been reflected in the creation of associations to support professional staff members with responsibility for managing fundraising programs. This includes the Association of Fundraising Professionals (AFP), originally founded as the National Society of Fund Raisers, which provides training and certification of members. The Council for Advancement and Support of Education (CASE) offers training, collects and publishes data, and establishes standards for the management of fundraising and related activities in colleges and universities, including institutionally related foundations. The Association of Governing Boards of Universities and Colleges (AGB) establishes and promotes standards for the governance of universities and the organization BoardSource does so for the broader nonprofit sector. As public school education foundations have increased in number and importance, they likewise have come to require professional management and standards of best practice.

Incorporated in 2021, the National Association of Education Foundations (NAEF) in 2024 included 1,360 individual members, serving 640 education foundations. The NAEF provides training, including an annual conference, and virtual networking and training webinars. It also provides certification of foundation managers as Certified Education Foundation Leaders. The National School Foundation Association, Inc. (NSFA) is the charitable arm for NAEF and raises funds to support the growth of foundations and programs that serve foundation staff. In order to establish standards for foundation practice, NAEF has developed Guiding Principles in four broad areas and nine sub-categories, as summarized in Box 1.1.

In addition to NAEF, there are various state associations of educational foundations. For example, the Indiana Association of Public Education Foundations serves 70 foundations across the state, providing "education, training, collaboration and advocacy to enhance public education." (Indiana Association, 2024) In Texas, the Texas Education Foundation Network (TEFN) is a program of the private Texas Pioneer Foundation and provides networking opportunities, sharing of best practices, training, and other resources to advance the work of local education foundations(Texas Education Foundation Network, n.d.).

Foundation Governance

The boards of public school education foundations are responsible for the organizations they govern, including the legal responsibilities of care, loyalty, and obedience that apply to all nonprofit boards. Both CASE and AGB provide programs and materials regarding the governance and operation of university-related foundations, with AGB being especially engaged with the topic. Some state associations of public school education foundations and NAEF have developed important resources, which are not yet as extensive as those addressing foundations in public universities.

Box 1.1 National Association of Education Foundations Guiding Principles: The Fundamentals

Transparency & Purpose

Stakeholder Identification

Advocacy

Accountability

Fund Development & Gift Stewardship

Financial Responsibility

Roles & Responsibilities

Endowment Management

Legal Governance & Organizational Development

District Relationships

Foundation Grantmaking

Professional Staff & Resources

Programs

Purpose

Research-Based Allocations

Community Responsiveness

Source: National Association of Education Foundations, Inc. (2025). Education Foundation Guiding Principles. Provided in email to author from Mike Taylor, chair, NAEF, June 24, 2025. Used with permission.

In a chapter written for a 2019-book focused on fundraising and institutional advancement in higher education, James H. Moore Jr., president of the University of Illinois Foundation, offered principles for building effective foundations supporting public universities, which may apply as well to public school education foundations (Moore, 2019). Moore emphasizes the importance of recognizing the fact that the purpose of the foundation is only to support the institution with which it is affiliated and develop a well-defined working relationship between the foundation and the institution. He also emphasizes the uniqueness of every institution and the need to shape the foundation's programs accordingly. Moore notes that some universities have multiple affiliated organizations, which may include alumni associations and foundations with specialized roles, such as supporting research. Understanding and managing relationships among these organizations is also essential to assure coordinated efforts and successful fundraising. With regard to foundation governance, Moore emphasizes the importance of maintaining the legal distinction between the foundation and the institution served and managing the relationship between the foundation's board and the institution's governing board. In the case of public schools, that would generally include an elected or an appointed school board as well as other governmental agencies that have a role in education.

In a book published by AGB, Michael Worth (2012) discusses the responsibilities of foundation boards in higher education. Like Moore, Worth observes the importance of maintaining relationships between the foundation board and the governing board of the public institution it serves, with the university governing board responsible for academic priorities and the foundation board responsible for raising and managing private funds to support those priorities. He also emphasizes the importance of the foundation board's involvement in fundraising.

Fundraising for Public Schools

While many people may think of fundraising for schools in terms of traditional events like bake sales or car washes, some public school education foundations have developed more comprehensive fundraising programs, resembling those found in universities. Such programs include a staff position titled vice president for development and directors assigned to managing specific programs or constituencies, such as annual giving, corporate support, foundation relations, and planned giving. While the scale of public school education foundations does not match those of large universities, higher education may provide useful lessons and models.

Fundraising is a major endeavor for universities, including public institutions. University fundraising has become a highly organized and professionalized activity, with some development staffs numbering in the hundreds. As discussed previously, fundraising by independent universities has centuries of history, while public universities have expanded their programs significantly in recent decades. Although some public universities can spend institutional resources on fundraising and receive gifts directly, most work with an institutionally related foundation. The advantages of doing so include more autonomy and flexibility in managing philanthropic funds and generating sufficient resources to meet fundraising costs. There is an extensive literature regarding fundraising practices and annual surveys that collect detailed data on giving, both in higher education and the broader nonprofit sector.

Total philanthropic giving in the United States totaled more than $557 billion in 2023. Of that total, 75 percent was given by individuals, including $374 billion by living individuals and $43 billion through bequests. While private foundations and corporate donors often gain high visibility, private foundations accounted for 19 percent and corporations only 7 percent of total giving in the United States in 2023 (Giving USA, 2024). However, it is important to emphasize that philanthropy totals do not capture all funding relationships involving corporations and nonprofit organizations. There are various forms of cause marketing relationships that provide support to nonprofits, the revenue from which is not classified as charitable since the corporate partners also receive some benefit. Some nonprofit organizations, including university-related foundations, have commercial and entrepreneurial partnerships with corporations. Religion is the largest recipient of giving, accounting for 24 percent of the total in 2023, with education and human services each accounting for 14 percent of the total (Giving USA, 2024).

The Council for Advancement and Support for Education (CASE) collects data on giving to higher education institutions and publishes the annual CASE Insights on Voluntary Support of Education. Beginning in 2022, CASE partnered with the National Association of Independent Schools to collect giving data published as CASE Insights on Philanthropy in Independent Schools. More than 1,400 independent schools participated in the 2023 survey and reported a total of $4.87 billion in gifts received in 2022 (CASE, 2024). However, at the time of this writing, CASE did not collect such data on giving to public school education foundations, so the total and sources of such support are not identified on a national basis.

Successful fundraising requires a team effort, including the board, chief executive officer, and fundraising professionals. Michael Worth (2012) describes their partnership using the metaphor of a football team. Members of the foundation board are the team owners. In that role, they have responsibility for assuring the foundation's adherence to legal and ethical standards, approving its broad strategies, and evaluating its performance. The board should not be calling specific plays — that is the responsibility of the coach. In other words, the foundation chief executive officer. But the owners hire the coach and may need to review that person's performance based on results, which may be defined by the win-loss record or, in the case of a foundation, fundraising success.

However, unlike football, in the game of fundraising it is not sufficient for the owners to merely observe the game from their skyboxes. Because they are leaders in their communities and thus credible advocates for the foundation and its purposes, they generally "are expected to play on the field, during the game, actively participating in running, blocking, passing, and scoring points (Worth, 2012, p. 57)." In other words, in order for the foundation to be successful, members of the foundation board must leverage their standing to engage others, open doors to potential donors and partners, and actively participate in the fundraising process.

As stated earlier, universities are different from public school districts in many ways. However, it is possible to find comparable points on which the literature regarding foundation governance and fundraising is applicable. The longer experience of foundations in higher education thus may help to inform public school education foundations as their importance continues to expand.

Building Effective Foundations

As explained in the introduction, this book is not intended to provide a comprehensive review of the research literature related to public school education foundations. Rather, it intends to be of practical interest to those foundations and their leaders by providing examples of current practices in governance, fundraising, grantmaking, and other aspects of foundation operation. However, some studies have addressed the characteristics of effective public school education foundations and their findings are worthy of consideration.

Some scholars have analyzed public data from foundations' Form 990s, while others have undertaken case studies, generally focusing on specific communities or states. Rikki Abzug and three co-authors (2016) looked at foundations in New Jersey to see what might explain higher levels of support on a per-student basis, which they defined as the measure of impact. Their findings suggested that the level of support received by the foundations was not significantly correlated with median income in the district, nor with other district characteristics, such as racial diversity, student test scores, and urbanization. The most significant variable associated with higher foundation funding was indeed the age of the foundation. As they explain, "established, legitimized community fixtures are able to attract, and then distribute, more money than newer, untested organizations" (p. 145).

In a study of 256 education foundations in Texas, Natalie Green Clogston (2021) found that the level of funding provided by foundations was not necessarily related to low government funding or racial diversity within the district. Characteristics associated with successful fundraising included the longevity of the foundation, the district's size and location, and community wealth. In addition, when Clogston looked at foundation practices, successful foundations were those that had paid staff, strong board composition, alignment with the school district's priorities, and engaged superintendents. When Clogston interviewed school superintendents, 100 percent agreed on the central importance of these practices. With regard to board composition, Clogston concluded that a governing board representative of the community is essential for "credibility, policy making, and fundraising." (p. 18). She agreed with Abzug et al. that the impact of funding provided by the foundations she studied was "nominal" if measured against total school budgets, but she also acknowledged that there are non-monetary benefits that come from having a foundation, including community engagement and advocacy.

In her doctoral dissertation, Heather M. Allen studied foundations in Virginia (Allen, 2014). Her findings generally agreed with those of Abzug and her colleagues (2016) and with those of Clogston's (2021). A foundation's longevity is related to its ability to raise funds, as are larger boards and the employment of professional foundation staff. Similar to Clogston

(2021), she concluded that the composition of foundation boards may be a predictor of fundraising success, with boards that are representative of the community being associated with greater support. She agreed that the relationship between the foundation and the school district, especially the superintendent, is related to success.

Leaving aside conditions that foundations are unable to control, such as their longevity and characteristics of the district that they serve, there is considerable consensus regarding the best practices that may lead to success: build a paid staff; enlist a strong board that is representative of the community; align the foundation's fundraising priorities with those of the district; and engage the superintendent in the foundation's activities. The case studies in this book explore these points and others.

Some researchers have focused on the question of whether public school education foundations are effective and have an impact. Effectiveness is generally defined as an organization achieving its objectives, while impact relates to whether it makes a difference in the broader world. It is important to clarify that both concepts are different than efficiency, which relates to the resources expended to achieve results.

With regard to public school education foundations, impact often has been defined by financial metrics. In a series of annual studies, since discontinued, consultant Dewey Caruthers of the Caruthers Institute developed a ranking of "top K-12 education foundations," which was published online under the title, *Stepping Up*. Caruthers identified the "top 50" foundations, based on data obtained from Form 990s (Ditmer, 2024). The eight metrics on which Caruthers based his rankings included annual revenues, revenues per student, total assets, assets per student, investment income, total program expenses, expenses per student, and volunteers (Ditmer, 2024). As Caruthers explained his definition of impact, "Per student calculations are [included] to better reveal the impact a foundation is having based on the number of students in the district. Some foundations raise large amounts of money but when compared to the number of students in their districts it becomes clear the impact on most students is minimal" (Caruthers, 2017).

Studies looking at financial metrics have concluded that the level of philanthropic funds raised by public school education foundations is insufficient to replace public funding for basic operating support. And, as mentioned previously, Rikki Abzug and her co-authors (2016) as well as Natalie Green Clogston (2021) also concluded that the totals raised were not sufficient to be significant. However, adopting the margin-for-excellence perspective explained earlier in this chapter suggests that financial metrics alone may not answer the question of whether foundations are making a difference in the school districts where they operate. That may require digging a little deeper into what kinds of programs and initiatives they support, exploring what innovations they pioneer, and evaluating foundation programs in terms of outcomes, that is, the changes expected to result from program initiatives. For example, that could mean innovations that achieve higher students test scores, improved school attendance, increased college admissions, and similar measures and then become models for wider adoption by the school system. Evaluating the impact of public school education foundations from this perspective would require going beyond overall financial metrics to evaluate the success of particular initiatives and the extent to which they have led to reforms that subsequently improved educational outcomes for larger numbers of students. As the case studies in following chapters describe, some foundations have undertaken significant efforts to evaluate their performance in this way.

About the Case Studies

The case studies presented in the following chapters of this book are based on available public information and interviews with foundation officers. The cases were designed to provide insights on many of the points discussed in this chapter, including: the origins and history of the foundation; staffing and operations; the fundraising program and philanthropic support; the foundation's board and governance; school programs and initiatives supported; the relationship between the foundation and the school district; and the definition of impact and methods of evaluation that are applied. Foundation executives who were interviewed also were asked to identify trends and issues affecting their own foundations and public school education foundations generally. It is hoped that the case studies will be of interest and value to those working to grow and strengthen public school education foundations across the country. In addition, some of the lessons they provide, which are summarized in the concluding chapter of this book, may have value for those who establish policy and lead school districts, including school boards, superintendents, and other officials.

References

Abzug, R., Olbrecht, A., Sabrin, M., & DeLeon, E. 2016. Nonprofit financing to the rescue? The slightly twisted case of local education foundations in New Jersey. *Nonprofit and Voluntary Sector Quarterly*, 45(1), pp. 133–149.

Allen, H.M. 2014. Public school foundations' support of K-12 public schools divisions in Virginia. Doctoral dissertation, Virginia Polytechnic Institute and State University.

Association of Governing Boards of Universities and Colleges (AGB). 2020. Institutionally related foundations. Accessed June 24, 2024. https://agb.org/knowledge-center/institutions/foundations/

Ballotpedia. n.d. Public school districts (United States). Accessed December 6, 2024. https://ballotpedia.org/Public_school_district_(United_States)

Caruthers, D. 2017. Stepping up: The nation's top K-12 education foundations. Accessed June 22, 2024. https://resources.finalsite.net/images/v1655151060/bhisd/tnoyictmzvlixycvbyot/Caruthers2017Rankings.pdf.

Clogston, N. G. 2021. The influence of private contributions in public education: An examination of education foundations. Dissertation, University of Houston-Clear Lake.

Council for Advancement and Support of Education (CASE). n.d. College and university foundations. Accessed June 24, 2024. https://www.case.org/connect/college-and-university-foundations#:~:text=The%20first%20college%20and%20university,established%20college%20and%20university%20foundations.

Council for Advancement and Support of Education (CASE) 2024. CASE Insights on Philanthropy in Independent Schools (United States). Accessed December 20, 2024. https://www.case.org/system/files/media/inline/CASE%20Insights%20Philanthropy%20in%20Independent%20Schools%202023.pdf

DC Public Education Fund. 2024. The intersection of philanthropy, innovation, and public school transformation. Accessed December 18, 2024. https://dcedfund.org/about/.

Ditmer, S. 2024. Study announces top 50 K-12 education foundations in the nation. Nebraska Association of Public Schools Foundations. Accessed November 4, 2024. https://napsf.org/news-events/foundations-in-action/study-announces-top-50-k-12education-foundations-in-the-nation.html

Fensterwald, J. 2022, June 2. California Prop. 13's "unjust legacy" detailed in critical study. *EdSource*. Accessed October 31, 2024. https://edsource.org/2022/californias-prop-13s-unjust-legacy-detailed-in-critical-study/674412

Fund for New York City Public Schools. n.d. Our mission and impact. Accessed April 18, 2025. https://www.fundfornycps.org/mission

Fund for the School District of Philadelphia. 2024. Opportunity to build. Accessed December 18, 2024. https://www.thefundsdp.org/what-we-do/.
Giving USA: The Annual Report on Philanthropy. 2024. Giving USA Foundation, The Giving Institute, and the Indiana University Lilly Family School of Philanthropy.
Haddad, D. 2022, May 13. The importance of public school educational foundations. *NonProfitPRO*. Accessed November 1, 2024. https://www.nonprofitpro.com/post/the-importance-of-public-school-educational-foundations/
Indiana Association of Public Education Foundations. 2024. Website. Accessed November 4, 2024. https://www.inapef.org/
Moore, J. H., Jr. 2019. Institutionally related foundations in public colleges and universities. In Worth, M. J. & M. T. Lambert, *Advancing higher education: New strategies for fundraising, philanthropy, and engagement*. Rowman & Littlefield, pp. 197–210.
National Association of Education Foundations, Inc. (2025). Education Foundation Guiding Principles. Provided in email to author from Mike Taylor, chair, NAEF, June 24, 2025.
National Association of State Universities and Land Grant Colleges, Office of Institutional Research. 1961, October. Margin for excellence. The Role of Voluntary Support in Public Higher Education. Accessed June 24, 2024. https://eric.ed.gov/?id=ED029571
National Center for Education Statistics (NCES). 2022. Enrollment, poverty, and federal funds for the 120 largest school districts, by enrollment size in 2021: School year 2019–20 and fiscal year 2022. Accessed November 3, 2024. https://nces.ed.gov/programs/digest/d22/tables/dt22_215.30.asp
Nelson, A. A. & Gazley, B. 2014. The rise of school-supporting nonprofits. *Education Finance and Policy*, (4), pp. 541–566.
Nisbet, E. 2021. Local-level philanthropic partnerships in public education: Dilemmas for equity and public responsibility. *Journal of Urban Affairs*, 43(2), pp. 251–269.
Richards, E. 2016, November 27. Revamped MPS Foundation sets new goals. *Milwaukee Journal Sentinel*. Accessed November 4, 2024. https://www.jsonline.com/story/news/education/2016/11/27/revamped-mps-foundation-sets-new-goals/94435898/
San Francisco Education Fund. n.d. Website. Accessed December 19, 2024. https://sfedfund.org/
Texas Education Foundation Network (TEFN). n.d. About us. Accessed December 18, 2024. https://www.tefn.org/about-us/
Worth, M. J. 2012. *Foundations for the future: The fundraising role of foundation boards at public colleges and universities*. Association of Governing Boards of Universities and Colleges.

2 Knox Education Foundation

Knox County is the geographical center of the Great Valley of East Tennessee, having a population of more than 432,000. Created in 1792, the county is named for Henry Knox, the first US Secretary of War. The county seat is Knoxville, the third largest city in Tennessee (Knox County, 2025). Knoxville is home to the University of Tennessee and emphasizes its quality of life, pleasant climate, and natural amenities (Knox County Schools, 2025).

Knox County Schools is a unified school district, enrolling more than 60,000 students, with more than 11 percent classified as living in poverty (NCES, 2024). The district is governed by an elected school board and managed by the superintendent of schools, who at the time of this writing was Dr. Jon Rysewyk. However, the district does not have taxing authority and is funded through appropriations from the county government. In addition to traditional public schools, the district included one public charter school at the time of writing this book, with a second one having been authorized.

Knox Education Foundation History and Overview

The Knox Education Foundation (KEF) provides support only for the public schools in the district, with the charter school having its own fundraising capability (Taylor, 2025). The KEF was created by the merger of two overlapping organizations in 2020 to serve as "a catalyst for transforming public education to achieve excellent outcomes for all students [and to provide] opportunities for businesses, community leaders, funders, and stakeholders to directly impact public education" (KEF, 2025). It defines its role in five areas:

Convener: Bringing stakeholders together to address common goals and find solutions for the challenges faced by our public education system.

Catalyst: Sparking innovation and advancing bold ideas to foster a culture of continuous improvement in public education.

Champion and Cheerleader: Celebrating successes, recognizing accomplishments, and building awareness.

Connector: Engaging communities, matching needs, raising funds, and facilitating investments.

Critical Friend: Addressing tough barriers to student achievement and shining light on issues of importance. (KEF, 2025)

The KEF is independent of Knox County Schools and local government does not have any control or veto power over its initiatives. However, the school system, city and county government represent five votes of sixteen members on the foundation's board of directors. The bylaws provide automatic appointments for the Knox County mayor, Knoxville City mayor, the chair of the Knox County Commission, the chair of the Board of Education, and the superintendent of schools. Until June 2023, the City of Knoxville, Knox County and Knox County Schools all provided funding to the foundation. As of 2025, only Knox County government provided funding to the foundation.

The foundation maintains a close relationship with the school district. Its offices are housed in the school district headquarters building and there are regular meetings between the foundation's chief executive officer and the superintendent to discuss the district's priorities and strategies (Taylor, 2025) The KEF was established through a merger of two pre-existing organizations, the Great Schools Partnership and Project GRAD Knoxville. There was an overlap between the programs of the two predecessor organizations, suggesting benefits of a merger. A further concern was the legal status of the Great Schools Partnership as a charitable trust, complicating the tax deductibility of gifts. The COVID-19 pandemic presented a challenge in the early days of the new foundation and some aspects of the transition were still underway in early 2025, when this case study was undertaken (Taylor, 2025).

Mike Taylor, the foundation's second chief executive officer as of early 2025, is a native of East Tennessee and joined the foundation in 2023 with more than thirty years in nonprofit management and fundraising. He previously served as CEO of the Henrico Education Foundation in Richmond, Virginia and Executive Director of the Mountain Education Foundation in Signal Mountain, Tennessee. He was attracted to leading public school education foundations by his observation of their impact on schools attended by his own children. In addition to his leadership of the Knox Education Foundation, Taylor serves as chair of the National Association of Education Foundations (NAEF), working to bring common national standards to the field and provide training and certification to foundations' staff.

At the time of this writing, the KEF staff included nine individuals. As Taylor notes, the recruitment of fundraising staff is a particular challenge, both because of the overall high demand for individuals with such experience and the proximity of the University of Tennessee, with a large development operation (Taylor, 2025). In addition to its full-time staff, the foundation engages consultants and contractors for specialized work, including public relations and grant writing, permitting foundation staff to focus on building long-term relationships with donors (Taylor, 2025).

Governance and Board Role

The foundation is governed by a board that in 2025 included sixteen individuals (KEF, 2025). As mentioned previously, the board includes school district and public officials, who serve with a full vote. Mike Taylor explains that having school and public officials as voting members of a public school education foundation board is an unusual model, but reflects the role of the school district and county in creating the foundation. One of the foundation's predecessor organizations, the Great Schools Partnership (GSP), was established in 2005 as an outgrowth of Knox County's "Every School a Great School" symposium to align efforts by leaders from the public and private sectors. Local government provided significant funding to GSP as well as legal oversight of the organization, and that structure was carried over to the new entity.

In addition to the school and public officials, the foundation's governance committee identifies new board members from the community who possess required skills and may help in expanding the foundation's constituency. The president of the University of Tennessee system serves on the foundation board and has been helpful in establishing relationships with funders (Taylor, 2025).

Taylor sees benefits in having public and school district officials on the board. The school district does not have its own taxing authority, so having city and county officials engaged in discussing priorities and strategies may be beneficial. The foundation board provides a forum for such discussions. Taylor reports, "Tennessee has been a leader in post-secondary education and we're looking at how we become a leader in K-12 and Pre-K education." In addition, the public officials on the board bring visibility and, consistent with ethical guidelines, can introduce the foundation to potential donors and grantors (Taylor, 2025). However, Taylor also notes a shortcoming of the current model. The school board chair and county commission chair positions turn over annually, which can make it more challenging to maintain continuity in the board's deliberations.

Board members are expected to give personally and/or help the foundation secure funds, commonly known as a give-or-get approach. As Taylor (2025) explains, the board may help to convene conversations, even if they do not participate in soliciting the gift.

Fundraising and Philanthropy

The foundation had revenue of more than $4.8 million from the year 2023 (KEF Form 990, 2023). Sources included 40 percent from grants made by foundations and corporations, 39 percent from government grants, 14 percent from gifts made by individuals, and the balance from other sources (Taylor, 2025). Public funding includes an earmark from the county government. Corporate supporters are recognized on the foundation's website, but individual donors are not.

The chief executive officer is actively involved in fundraising and focuses his efforts on meeting with donors of larger gifts, while the chief development officer manages programs intended to secure a broader base of support. Increasing the base of individual donors is a current priority. The superintendent of schools often attends meetings with funders and explains the programs for which support is needed, but stops short of actually "making the ask" (Taylor, 2025).

Although KEF has sent some direct mail and email, fundraising from individuals has relied primarily on events that have included a daylong telethon conducted in partnership with a local television station and a back-to-school breakfast program, which produced some individual gifts. Taylor emphasizes that the foundation was established in 2020 and is not yet well-known among all members of the community. Events thus have a dual purpose of raising visibility and awareness as well as engaging new donors.

Programs and Impact

The KEF has defined five focus areas for its work: investing in talent and conducting research in overall third-grade reading proficiency; overall middle school math proficiency; enrollment in higher education, credentialing programs, or armed services; access to quality Pre-K; and recruitment and retention of effective educators (KEF, 2025). The foundation maintains ongoing programs and also provides one-time grants for projects intended to improve student outcomes. Box 1.1 includes a summary of initiatives identified on the Foundation's website at the time of this writing.

Mike Taylor (2025) explains that the foundation has moved away from providing ongoing services directly. For example, it transferred a community schools initiative to United Way. It emphasizes priority-based grants to support innovative initiatives designed to improve student outcomes and perhaps establish a new approach for adoption across the school system. If innovations funded by the foundation prove to be effective, it may help make the case for including new programs in the school district budget. As Taylor explains, "We're not just here to write checks to the district. We're here to help improve student outcomes, get innovative things into the classroom, and then figure out how we can address barriers and systems that don't work well." He adds,

> What better way for the school board to make the case to the county commission for funding? We can fund pilot initiatives, then take the data and outcomes to argue for the adoption of new approaches. If there are improved student outcomes, on-time graduation has increased, reading scores have improved, whatever it is, that strengthens the case for why these approaches should be replicated across the district (Taylor, 2025).

These initiatives are what Taylor refers to as "systems change" initiatives (Taylor, 2025). As he points out, the foundation is not "chasing money for the sake of money." Instead, fundraising and the initiatives prioritized for funding must prove to be "impactful to the school district" (Taylor, 2025).

In some instances, KEF funds the work of consultants to help develop strategies for the schools. For example, the foundation funded a project conducted by Ford Next Generation Learning to identify community needs and assist the school district in "reimaging the high school experience" (Taylor, 2025). The result was design of the 865 Academies, of which the foundation was the convening organization and original funder (Taylor, 2025). The program engages students with businesses, organizations, and other partners to explore post-high school opportunities, including higher education, enlisting in service to their country, and high-skill, high-wage employment (KEF, 2025).

Knox County Schools has defined five regions and established regional teams that include a director and supervisor—one with elementary experience and the other with secondary experience—and additional members with expertise in various content areas. Schools are assigned to the five regions based on feeder patterns and geographic proximity (Knox County Schools, 2025). Region 5, which encompasses downtown Knoxville, includes many schools facing challenges. The KEF funded a consultant to assist the school district in developing a plan for Region 5. The result was a strategic plan that emphasized improving third-grade reading levels, improving on-time graduation rates, and creating additional pre-K seats. The plan includes performance metrics that are reviewed quarterly (Taylor, 2025).

The foundation emphasizes outcomes in programs where they can be evaluated, for example, in its priority-based grants, and has established a full-time staff position dedicated to evaluation. It also maintains a relationship with the Boyd Center at the University of Tennessee, which assists with collecting and analyzing information to compare census and school data. Mike Taylor (2025) expresses the hope that some of this data and school system data may eventually be made available on publicly available dashboards.

Box 2.1 Knox Education Foundation Initiatives

865 Academies

KEF is the convening organization supporting Knox County Schools with the reimagination of the high school experience through The 865 Academies. KEF supports the initiative by recruiting and cultivating collaborative and academy-aligned businesses, organizations, and industry partnerships for student experiences and post-high school opportunities.

One Book Read City

KEF facilitates One Book Read City, a community-wide literacy initiative that engages all Knox County elementary school students through two weeks of captivating events and activities centered around a thoughtfully selected book. It brings together businesses, non-profit organizations, and schools for a unified effort to support literacy.

Playspace Fund

KEF has created a private-public fund to help reverse three decades of challenges for our public schools and reinforce the importance of play for our students. This innovative funding solution will support playspaces across Knox County Schools.

Priority-Based Grants

KEF provides grants across multiple levels that support projects that accelerate student learning, address a challenge, or promote innovative ideas. These projects align with the four priority areas of Knox County Schools and have measurable outcomes.

Project GRAD

Project GRAD provides community and family resources to help ensure successful transition to post-secondary enrollment and supporting scholar completion through efforts to inform, equip, and support graduates from Austin-East and Fulton high schools.

SOURCE: KEF. 2025. Our initiatives. Accessed January 25, 2025.

https://www.knoxed.org/initiatives/. Used with permission.

What if an innovation is not productive? Taylor observes that even such an experience can be useful: "It's okay because we had an idea and we learned that it didn't work or didn't accomplish what we'd hoped. But that informs future decisions. We'll fund things that show the best results."

In addition to providing financial support, the Foundation engages in advocacy on behalf of Knox County Schools. Taylor (2025) emphasizes that the foundation does not engage in lobbying, but it is a resource for the community and school board. He meets regularly with the school board and with individual members to provide information about the foundation's activities and learn more about the district's needs. On some occasions, the foundation serves to communicate with the public about the school system. As Taylor (2025) observes, "there are times that a foundation can share a message or get out in front of something when it would be harder for a superintendent or school district to do that."

Trends and Challenges

Speaking with the authors in 2025, Mike Taylor observed trends and challenges facing public schools generally, the KEF in particular, and public school education foundations across the country. Teacher retention is a challenge for many school districts, a problem that became acute during the COVID-19 pandemic and is still persisting. Another concern is third-grade reading, with many schools experiencing deficits that need to be addressed. The State of Tennessee has not increased funding for Pre-K services, such as child care recently, which, as shown by evidence, is important for schools' success. Taylor (2025) sees a need to address basics, referring to as "blocking and tackling." He observes, "You can't really innovate until you've got a qualified, well-trained teacher in the classroom every day who is supported." Through its funding and advocacy initiatives, the KEF strives to address such issues in dialog with the school district and public and private partners.

With regard to KEF, Taylor cites challenges in hiring and retaining professional staff, who are essential to advancing the foundation's work. The University of Tennessee and other nonprofit organizations compete for talent. Knoxville is a substantial but not large city and thus has a limited pool of individuals with the necessary experience. Balancing the foundation's relationship with the school board can sometimes be complicated and the foundation's advocacy efforts must navigate around continuing debates concerning charter schools, voucher programs, and other issues related to public education.

At the time of his discussion with the authors in 2025, Taylor also served as chair of the National Association of Education Foundations (NAEF). That role provided him with a perspective going beyond his own school district and foundation. Trends he observed in the management of foundations include an emphasis on establishing standards of practice and increasing professionalization of foundation staff through training and certification provided by NAEF. He emphasized that foundation officers need to understand governance, fundraising, and the process of navigating the complexities of laws and policies in their individual states.

The use of data to evaluate programs and plan new initiatives also is growing. As Taylor observes, fundraising for schools once was done primarily by volunteers, for example, members of PTAs. As it becomes professionalized in foundations and the magnitude of foundation funding grows, there is an increasing need for data both to guide efforts and report back to funders on the impact of their support. Taylor notes that many public school education foundations serve small districts; and maintaining a benefits program for staff can be difficult. Staff members at some foundations can participate in the school district's plan but others are unable to do so. The NAEF is developing a program to assist small foundations in meeting that need.

Summarizing the role of public school education foundations, Taylor (2025) observes that they exist in a more complex environment than most nonprofit organizations, since they are working for change and progress in educational programs that they do not control. "We navigate not just the nonprofit sector, but also the public sector," he observes, adding "Foundations bring in money for schools from the private sector, but they also help the private sector understand the intricacies of public schools, which involve local, state, and national processes that must be navigated to bring change."

References

Knox County. 2025. Website. Accessed January 23, 2025. https://www.knoxcounty.org/

Knox County Schools. 2025. About. Accessed January 23, 2025. https://www.knoxschools.org/Page/5649

KEF (Knox Education Foundation). 2025. Website. Accessed January 23, 2025. https://www.knoxed.org/

KEF (Knox Education Foundation). 2023. Form 990. Accessed January 25, 2025. https://projects.propublica.org/nonprofits/organizations/621865303/202313189349311641/full

NCES (National Center for Education Statistics). 2024. Enrollment, poverty, and federal funds for the 120 largest school districts, by enrollment size in 2021: School year 2019–20 and fiscal year 2022. Accessed November 7, 2024. https://nces.ed.gov/programs/digest/d19/tables/dt19_215.30.asp
Taylor, Mike. 2025. Interview with authors January 23, 2025.

3 DC Public Education Fund

Washington, District of Columbia (DC), is the capital of the United States, established as the seat of the national government in 1790. The District of Columbia is not a state and the United States Congress retains ultimate control of the city's budget. However, local citizens were granted the right to elect a school board in 1970 and the Home Rule Act of 1973 delegated more authority to local government, including an elected mayor and city council (Council of the District of Columbia, 2016).

The structure of the DC Public Schools is complex. The mayor has full authority over traditional public schools in the District, subject to budget and performance oversight from the elected city council. That includes appointment of the chancellor, the chief executive officer of the school system, who at the time of this writing was Dr. Lewis D. Ferebee. Charter schools are governed by the independent DC Public Charter School Board, members of which are nominated by the mayor, with the advice and consent of the DC City Council (DC State Board of Education, 2023). There are 117 public schools across the district, enrolling more than 51,000 students of diverse racial and ethnic backgrounds (District of Columbia Public Schools, 2024).

DC Public Education Fund History and Overview

The DC Public Education Fund was founded in 2007 as an independent organization, but with encouragement from the then school chancellor Michelle Rhee, who had a background in philanthropy and believed that private support could have an impact. The Fund defines its role in three key areas (DC Public Education Fund, 2025):

- Making ambitious investments
- Developing thoughtful partnerships
- Demonstrating proven results

The Fund describes its work as "[raising] significant private dollars that incubate cutting-edge start-up ideas for students. We are DCPS' very own venture fund" (DC Public Education Fund, 2025). The Fund provides support only for initiatives in traditional public schools, with charter schools conducting their own fundraising.

Although independent, the Fund works closely with the DC Public Schools. Although no school officials serve on its board, the chancellor and other school district leaders attend meetings of the Fund's board and engage in discussions. The chancellor presents the state of the schools to the board and does an overview of the metrics of key data points related to programs that the Fund is supporting. The Fund's president and executive director also meets regularly with school officials outside of board meetings. However, as of 2025, the Fund has not created a separate strategic plan; rather, it takes its lead from the school district's five-year capital commitment plan and "works with the district, the chancellor, and the chancellor's team to identify what role public private partnerships may play in implementing the district's plan" (Kline, 2025).

Jim Kline joined the Fund as president and executive director in 2022. Kline began his career by joining Teach for America following his graduation from Rutgers University and was assigned to a school in New Orleans. He remained in New Orleans as a teacher, administrator, and coach for nine years, where he came to understand the potential impact of philanthropy in public education. He explains, "I saw the need for more support for our teachers, stronger professional development, stronger coaching. And I think the reason I wanted to become involved in education philanthropy was because it played a big role in my life" (Kline, 2025). He later moved to a foundation in Philadelphia that supported education and eventually to the DC Public Education Fund. At the time of this writing, the Fund employed a staff of six individuals, with the number varying from year-to-year depending on the number of active grants that need to be managed (Kline, 2025).

Jim Kline views the DC Education Fund as distinct among public school education foundations, in part because of the city's unusual characteristics. While Washington is a major city, its public school system is smaller than those in many other cities. For that reason, it is an effective proving ground for testing innovations and demonstrating results, then helping other cities adopt them. As he explains, "It is a fertile ground for really proving new ideas that work and scaling those in a way that might be difficult to do in a larger district" (Kline, 2025). That reality has been recognized by national foundations, who "view us as a place that really can help show others how to do new things in education" (Kline, 2025).

Governance and Board Role

The Fund's board is self-perpetuating and included eight individuals as of the time of this writing. There are no members who are school officials or who hold ex-officio appointments. The board does not have a requirement for board giving or fundraising by its members, although some do give personally and help connect the Fund with other sources of support. Board members also provide insights and advice in their areas of strength, for example, in communications, finance, and other areas. There is an intentional effort to fill gaps in the board's expertise by recruiting individuals who bring needed skills.

Fundraising and Philanthropy

The Fund had total gift and grant revenue of almost $15 million in 2022 (DC Public Education Fund Form 990, 2023). Its sources of support reflect its mission. It does not directly manage programs on an ongoing basis, but rather defines itself as "an agent of research and development, an agent of innovation" (Kline, 2025). As Kline describes, the Fund operates like "an R&D engine," using private funds to test innovations that the school district may then adopt in its ongoing operations, making it attractive to many national foundations interested in educational innovation. Although percentages somewhat vary from year to year, foundation grants comprise 80% or more of revenue, with corporate grants being the second largest source. Individual donors have provided a relatively small percentage of the fund's revenue, although Jim Kline reports that efforts are being made to diversify revenue sources, including a greater emphasis on individuals. The Fund's annual Standing Ovation event, which honors teachers, school leaders, and school communities, is a principal venue for identifying potential individual donors (Kline, 2025).

Jim Kline (2025) sees the involvement of corporations as having value beyond the dollars they provide. He explains,

> Across the nation, people don't necessarily view our public schools and our teachers in the most positive way. A great thing that happens when we connect more with corporations is that they are able to see the excellent work that's happening in our schools and they're seeing the bright spots. That helps the schools with overall community relations, which I think is deeply important.

The president and executive director is frequently engaged in meetings with donors and the Fund's staff includes a manager of fundraising programs. The board does not include a standing committee on fundraising, but it has established ad-hoc committees to focus on fundraising plans.

Programs and Impact

As mentioned previously, the DC Public Education Fund does not manage or support ongoing programs, but rather functions more as a funder of new ideas. Its initiatives are intended to test innovative approaches that may subsequently be adopted by the DC Public Schools or other districts. Table 3.1 includes, as examples, some initiatives identified on the Fund's website in early 2025, as updated by the Fund for this case study.

The Fund looks to school leaders to identify needs and propose initiatives. It then evaluates the potential for gaining funding and making the program sustainable. "We want something that is heavy on the startup costs and shows a path for sustainability," Kline (2025) explains, "We don't want funders to be approached for anything that doesn't on its face look like it's ultimately sustainable."

Box 3.1 DC Public Education Fund Current Priorities

Reimagining Math Instruction

Recognizing the urgent need for academic recovery and excellence, the DC Ed Fund invests in math instructional initiatives that provide targeted interventions, high-quality curriculum support, and educator training. Programs like high-dosage tutoring aim to close learning gaps and advance student achievement, while engaging families in the math instructional experience.

Workforce Development & Career Pathways

The DC Ed Fund supports DCPS in developing workforce-aligned learning opportunities, ensuring students graduate ready for career and college. Through partnerships with industry leaders and local employers, students access career exposure, skills training, and certifications in high-demand fields, building pathways to economic mobility.

DC Reading Clinic

The DC Reading Clinic provides intensive, one-on-one support for struggling readers while also training educators to become literacy experts. The clinic operates in multiple locations across the city, helping students build strong foundational reading skills and fostering a district-wide culture of literacy excellence.

Beyond the Bell

Beyond the Bell expands access to youth sports, clubs, and immersive activities, enriching the middle school experience for DC Public School students. Aligned with DCPS's 2023–2028 Strategic Plan, this initiative doubles afterschool enrichment opportunities, fostering student growth, connection, and belonging. From robotics clubs to outdoor adventures, Beyond the Bell strengthens school communities and student engagement.

Older Grant Programs include: Equity-centered Leadership Development

The DC Ed Fund partners with universities and community organizations to strengthen DCPS's leadership pipeline, ensuring a diverse, equity-driven principal and educator workforce. This initiative supports aspiring leaders through professional development, mentorship, and strategic pathways to school leadership roles.

High School Transformation

The DC Ed Fund works alongside DCPS and national partners to redesign the high school experience, ensuring students receive relevant, engaging, and future-ready education. This includes innovations at schools like Anacostia and Ballou High Schools and collaboration with Bard Early College to expand dual-enrollment opportunities.

DCPS Becoming

DCPS is committed to becoming a whole child-centered organization. This initiative focuses on fostering inclusive learning environments, advancing equity, and ensuring that every student feels loved, challenged, and prepared to thrive in an ever-evolving world. DCPS Becoming builds upon lessons learned in recent years to reshape teaching, learning, and school culture in a way that prioritizes student and educator well-being. Key outcomes of this work are ensuring our coming to school every day, valued and respected as whole people.

SOURCE: DC Public Education Fund. Email to authors from Jim Kline, February 19, 2025.

Used with permission.

One example of success is the DC Reading Clinic, a program launched in 2018 with start-up funding from foundations secured by the DC Public Education Fund. The clinic offers intense, one-on-one sessions for students struggling with reading and offers clinical apprenticeships to help educators become literacy experts. Because of its success, the school district began to provide regular funding for the clinic and had become the primary source of support by 2025, as the DC Public Education Fund began to conclude its involvement. Over five years of the clinic's operation, student reading scores increased 1.5 times, 100 percent of teachers who participated said they would recommend the program to their peers, and more than 10,000 students were impacted (DC Public Education Fund, 2025).

By 2025, the Fund was focusing its planning for new initiatives in two areas—"reimagining math" and "pathways," a program to help students identify their post-secondary directions (Kline, 2025). The COVID-19 pandemic caused a decline in student performance in mathematics, requiring new and extended efforts to recover. The DC Public Education Fund began pursuing programs to strengthen professional development for teachers, improved math curriculum and materials, and expand math tutoring for students. New efforts also were being explored to prepare public school students for post-secondary pathways. The purpose was to develop programs that offer counseling, internships, apprenticeships, and other programs to assist students in considering their future directions, whether for college or for direct entry into a professional field (Kline, 2025).

The Fund measures outcome metrics for all of its initiatives and also monitors two broader goals: making DC Public Schools "the best school district in the nation" and advancing equity, which Jim Kline (2025) calls "the civil rights issue of our time." Among the macro data that the Fund monitors are high school graduation rates and data obtained from the National Assessment of Educational Progress (NAEP), an assessment of mathematics and reading skills at the fourth and eighth grade levels provided by the National Center for Education Statistics. The data enable the Fund to determine how DC public schools are performing year-over-year against their own history, compared with other school districts, and with regard to various sub-groups of students. A third set of data that is monitored results from a panorama survey of all students in the district. As Jim Kline (2025) describes it,

> The panorama survey is a whole child survey. It asks students about whether they feel like they belong at school, do they feel safe, do they feel seen, do they feel like they're being prepared? It asks them questions around their experience at school. And the metric that we very closely consider and align with in terms of whether or not we're experiencing success is the belongingness score.

The Fund does not engage in advocacy or lobbying related to specific public policies, maintaining a conscious neutrality. Rather, it focuses on its specific initiatives and communicating the overall importance of public education.

Trends and Challenges

Jim Kline (2025) observes changes in philanthropy as a trend and also as a challenge to the DC Public Education Fund and the field generally. The passing of wealth to millennials, the move of some foundations to sunset their programs, and other changes that have occurred following the COVID-19 pandemic have made it more difficult to obtain support for new programs. Public school education foundation executives are now required to focus more on fundraising and are working to diversify their sources in view of the changing landscape.

Another trend and challenge is changing views of public education. That includes political debates about questions such as charter schools and voucher programs. Jim Kline (2025) notes that he is a supporter of charter schools, but he also believes that maintaining the quality of public schools is imperative, which involves moral questions.

Kline (2025) observes that a number of nonprofit organizations beyond public school education foundations also function as intermediaries, channeling philanthropic funds to public schools, often in support of specific issue areas. While acknowledging that some such organizations have been effective, he also speculates that some mergers among nonprofits might increase overall impact.

Expressing his commitment to the importance of public education and the role of organizations such as the DC Public Education Fund, Kline (2025) concludes that "We need to continue to fight for the future of public schools and explain why public education matters—to our democracy, to our workforce, to our mental health, to our students with disabilities, and to our students who don't have other options."

References

Council of the District of Columbia. 2016. D.C. home rule. Accessed January 27, 2025. https://dccouncil.gov/dc-home-rule/

DC Public Education Fund Form 990. 2023. Accessed February 6, 2025. https://projects.propublica.org/nonprofits/organizations/261607955/202432119349300528/full

DC Public Education Fund. 2025. Website. Accessed January 27, 2025. https://dcedfund.org/

DC State Board of Education Office of the Student Advocate. 2023. Understanding the DC public education landscape. Accessed January 27, 2025. https://studentadvocate.dc.gov/sites/default/files/dc/sites/studentadvocate.dc.gov/DC%20Governance%20Updated%202023%20%28Public%29%20%281%29.pdf

District of Columbia Public Schools. 2024. Fast facts. Accessed January 27, 2025. https://dcps.dc.gov/sites/default/files/dc/sites/dcps/publication/attachments/02.29.24%20DCPS%20Fast%20Facts.pdf

Kline, Jim. 2025. Interview with authors, February 3, 2025.

4 Greater Los Angeles Education Foundation

Los Angeles County, in California, is the largest and most diverse county in the nation, with a population of 10 million. The structure of its public schools is complex. The Los Angeles County Office of Education (LACOE) is the largest regional education agency in the United States, serving eighty school districts and more than 350 charter schools, with nearly two million students. The individual school districts range in size from the Los Angeles Unified School District (LAUSD), enrolling more than 557,000 students, to the Gorman School District, with just ninety (LAUSD, 2025a; California Department of Education, n.d.). The LAUSD is the nation's second largest school district, covering the city of Los Angeles as well as parts of twenty-five adjacent areas. In 2022, more than 21percent of students were from backgrounds defined as poverty (NCES, 2022).

The LACOE provides direct instruction to students in some specialized programs, for example, students enrolled in juvenile court schools, but its primary purpose is to support the various school districts within the county with specialized services and consultation (LACOE, n.d.). The county Board of Supervisors appoints the seven-member County Board of Education and the County Superintendent of Schools, who at the time of this writing was Dr. Debra Duardo (LACOE, 2024).

Greater Los Angeles Education Foundation History and Overview

The Greater Los Angeles Education Foundation (GLAEF) is the philanthropic partner of LACOE, created in 2019 as an outgrowth of a supporting organization named Friends of LACOE, at the initiative of the LA County

Superintendent of Schools, Dr. Debra Duardo. GLAEF's mission is "advancing deeper collaboration between schools and communities to disrupt inequity and meet the needs of today's diverse learners across Los Angeles County" (GLAEF 2024a). In 2022, GLAEF had revenues of almost $2.7 million and expenses of more than $2.2 million (GLAEF, 2022). Although GLAEF is an independent 501(c)(3) public foundation, its integration with LACOE requires that it also comply with California laws regarding transparency of public entities (Gelinas, 2025)

GLAEF's president and chief deputy of strategic partnerships and innovation, Kerry Lynn Franco, joined the foundation in 2022, having been recruited from a career in higher education, which included fundraising positions. Sam Gelinas, the foundation's vice president of programs, strategy, and development had served as acting executive director before Franco's appointment. Before coming to GLAEF, Gelinas held various positions in Los Angeles-area nonprofits and had begun his career as a special education teacher in Washington, DC. Both Franco and Gelinas spoke with the authors in March 2025.

Of the eighty school districts in Los Angeles County, about sixty-one have their own foundations serving the district. Some are relatively new, while others have a longer history than GLAEF. However, some of the district foundations are inactive. Superintendent Duardo moved to create GLAEF in order to expand the role of philanthropy and public-private partnerships throughout the county (Franco, 2025). Given the existence of foundations within individual districts, the role of the county-wide foundation requires definition. As Kerry Franco explains, "We fill the gaps for districts that do not have active foundations and support the foundations that are active. Our goal is to assure that no educational community is left behind" (Franco, 2025).

The GLAEF is closely integrated with the county's Board of Education and Superintendent of Schools, with school officials serving on the foundation's board and Franco serving as a member of the superintendent's cabinet. As Sam Gelinas describes, "every foundation project is developed in partnership with the LACOE team and with LACOE leadership" (Gelinas, 2025). In some instances, GLAEF makes grants that run through the foundations associated with individual school districts. In other instances, GLAEF and the district foundations work in partnership. As one example, Gelinas (2025) notes recovery efforts following devastating fires in the Los Angeles area in

2025. The GLAEF worked closely with the Pasadena Education Foundation to support affected students and teachers and assure that efforts were complementary.

Governance and Board Role

The GLAEF's board is composed of nine individuals, including the county Superintendent of Schools and members of the superintendent's staff, who serve as ex-officio members with a vote. Other members include community and business leaders, who serve three-year terms, which are renewable without limit.

The board's activity has become more structured and deliberate in recent years, with implementation of a give-or-get policy, a formal process for the selection of new board members, and an orientation process for new board members. Members of the foundation board meet annually with Kerry Franco to discuss their engagement for the coming year (Franco, 2025).

Fundraising and Philanthropy

Approximately 90 percent of GLAEF's funding comes from philanthropic foundations with an established interest in education, most of which have a regional focus. Sam Gelinas (2025) notes that while GLAEF does develop proposals for foundations, it also has ongoing relationships with some that see GLAEF as an effective vehicle for advancing their own programmatic objective. In some instances, those foundations are proactive in initiating projects. As he explains, "we can work with foundations that we know have priorities aligned with ours and that we can help to operationalize because of our affiliation with LACOE." Another 8–9 percent of revenue is provided by corporations, often in connection with event sponsorships, with only about 1 percent coming from individual donors (Gelinas, 2025).

Kerry Franco (2025) identifies increasing individual giving as an area of current emphasis. This is being pursued through a series of events intended to increase visibility and build relationships. A program for giving by LACOE employees and vendors has been developed. The foundation is utilizing social media to attract interest and participates in initiatives such as Giving Tuesday.

Programs and Impact

The GLAEF defines initiatives in five broad areas, as summarized in Box 4.1, including the LACOE Community Schools Initiative and programs intended to advance digital equity, support student-centered teaching and learning, strengthen college access and career pathways, and expand out-of-school learning and enrichment. It also works in regional partnerships with nonprofit service providers, government agencies, and cultural institutions to provide expanded learning opportunities for students.

Various projects and activities are encompassed under these umbrellas. For example, the community schools initiative provides professional development for school faculty and staff and the evaluation of pilot programs. The Foundation worked with LACOE to codify its community school model into a regional toolkit and provides technical assistance and support to help new schools adopt this framework (GLAEF, 2024b). The initiative to advance digital equity encompasses developing AI tools and guidelines for districts as well as the expansion of in-person brick and mortar tech centers for high school students. The student-centered teaching and learning initiative includes workforce development as well as regional research.

The evaluation of programs and projects is often defined by outcomes required by the terms of grants. Typical metrics include the number of students served and school performance. In some cases, GLAEF retains outside evaluators to compile data needed to complete evaluations. In the case of research supported by GLAEF, performance measures include the number of people who have downloaded reports or engaged with the research in other ways (Gelinas, 2025). Given its close relationship with LACOE, GLAEF does not engage in policy advocacy. However, Sam Gelinas (2025) notes that it may engage in "soft advocacy" by making recommendations based on research findings.

As a new organization and somewhat of a "blank slate," operating within a large regional education agency that does many different things, the Foundation has "struggled" with defining its programs (Gelinas, 2025). Although GLAEF has a strategic plan, Gelinas (2025) explains that it is still easy to get excited about new opportunities and "say yes to lots of different projects." However, due to the foundation's limited bandwidth and capacity, its leadership concentrates on instilling "guardrails" around priorities rather than going in too many different directions (Gelinas, 2025).

Box 4.1 Greater Los Angeles Education Foundation Programs And Initiatives

LACOE Community Schools Initiative

The LACOE Community Schools model is a poverty-mitigation strategy that consists of highly integrated District, LACOE, and County Agency services within schools. GLAEF has invested in the infrastructure needed to replicate the unique structure of LACOE's model, bringing services on-site and leveraging public funds.

Advancing Digital Equity

GLAEF is a Founding Partner of the LA Community Impact Hub, a unique network of creative spaces for teens to explore technology, build skills, and gain exposure to the regional employers in tech and entertainment. In addition to partners such as Best Buy Foundation™, the Annenberg Foundation, and Los Angeles County, we connect local youth with the careers of tomorrow - starting with the robust creative economy in Los Angeles County.

Student-Centered Teaching & Learning

GLAEF is focused on ensuring that all LA County Districts and schools have the resources and capacity to ensure that all students are able to thrive in college, career, and life.

College Access & Career Pathways

GLAEF is focused on strengthening postsecondary access, success, and transition supports for low-income and BIPOC high school students by expanding access to equitable and enhanced dual enrollment offerings....To facilitate lasting systemic change aimed at closing long-standing equity gaps and enhancing postsecondary and career technical education outcomes for historically underserved populations in Los Angeles County, GLAEF initiated a formal dual enrollment effort with the dedicated staff at LACOE....[to] foster collaboration [among] K-12 institutions, community colleges, [and] advising and advocacy organizations and [to] formulate equity-driven strategies to bolster dual enrollment programs across all districts and charter schools....

Expanded Learning, Enrichment & Partnerships
GLAEF is focused on the advancement of out-of-school learning time, school-day enrichment and expanded learning, which is critical in broadening students' horizons, cementing new concepts, and exposing youth to new opportunities.

Stitch
To help students have access to the vast network of enrichment services, GLAEF and a coalition of partners have developed Stitch. It is a searchable database profiling youth programming and services throughout LA County. It captures diverse organizations across all disciplines, program types, and focus areas that share the commitment of serving local youth.

Regional Partnerships
We work with a coalition of regional partners to develop new strategies to support district partnerships with non-profit service providers, aligned agencies, cultural institutions, and more to ensure all students have access to robust, dynamic, and diverse expanded learning opportunities.

Source: GLAEF, 2024b. Our work/programs and initiatives. Accessed February 24, 2025. https://www.glaef.org/. Adapted by the authors. Used with permission.

Trends and Challenges

Speaking in 2025, Sam Gelinas noted that GLAEF remained a young organization. Determining its priorities given its limited capacity has been a challenge. In addition, GLAEF's relationships with LACOE and district-level foundations have required attention.

As mentioned previously, some school districts in Los Angeles County have worked with their own education foundations for years, but philanthropy's role at the county level was not fully understood by all officials and staff at LACOE when GLAEF was established. As Gelinas (2025) explains, "helping them understand the benefits and resources we might provide has required some time and the building of relationships. We have needed to figure out how to position ourselves as a new institution working within an established institution, achieve some wins, and demonstrate our own sustainability. That just takes time." Kerry Franco (2025) observes, "School districts are public agencies, which face mandates. They are different from a foundation like ours. Our mission is to serve teachers and students, but our donors also are our constituents, so there is a need for dialog to gain understanding of our role." There also has been a need to define relationships between GLAEF and multiple district-level foundations and to develop frameworks for collaborative and complementary efforts.

Looking ahead, Kerry Franco (2025) places an emphasis on assuring GLAEF's own sustainability. That could include developing its endowment so that it can become a grant-maker in its own right, rather than only a strategic partner with LACOE. Funds received in 2024 established GLAEF's first endowment, designated to support students in the City of Inglewood ("Greater Los Angeles Education Foundation Establishes Over $12 Million Education Endowment Fund Supporting Youth in Inglewood, California," 2024). At the time of the authors' conversation with Franco and Gelinas, GLAEF was working out the details of its communications and grant-making strategy and hoping that the creation of additional endowment funds might help to advance its own sustainability and expand its role in the future.

Franco and Gelinas identify various trends and challenges shaping the future of public education and public school education foundations. Sam Gelinas (2025) observes that the most important trend is enrollment in public schools, which has declined in some areas. "Enrollment drives everything," he explains, "including district finance, district staffing, and district facilities." In addition, changing priorities in federal government policy could have an impact on public school systems across the country.

Kerry Franco notes the pressures facing many teachers and school administrators, which were exacerbated by the COVID-19 pandemic but continue. While philanthropy can play an important role in helping address resource constraints, managing external partnerships would add to the burdens on already-challenged school administrators. Having affiliated foundations with their own staff to manage those relationships helps avoid that added pressure. These are some of the reasons that Franco challenges existing thought processes to find new ways to bring philanthropy closer to those working within the environment on a daily basis. One of her strategies is to expand who is considered a constituent to those doing the work, the teachers. Franco's approach intends to break down silos and allow GLAEF to work more closely with those that it is serving. Franco (2025) points out that the way a foundation and a public agency think about funding is different, so coordination and collaboration is important to improve outcomes together. She further states, "We all believe in the same things."

While Kerry Franco sees an important role for public school education foundations in the future, she also observes a need for more collaboration among them. She has considered bringing foundation leaders together from across the state of California; and views national efforts, such as the National Association of Education Foundations, as essential to helping foundations meet the needs of public education in a time of growing challenges.

References

California Department of Education. n.d. School profile: Gorman Elementary. Accessed April 2, 2025. https://www.cde.ca.gov/sdprofile/details.aspx?cds=19645846013940

Franco, Kerry. 2025. Interview with authors. March 7, 2025.

Gelinas, Sam. 2025. Interview with authors. March 7, 2025.

GLAEF (Greater Los Angeles Education Foundation). 2022. Form 990. Accessed March 8, 2025. https://projects.propublica.org/nonprofits/organizations/474426889/202431309349300203/full

GLAEF (Greater Los Angeles Education Foundation). 2024b. Our work/programs and initiatives. Accessed February 24, 2025. https://www.glaef.org/programs-initiatives

Greater Los Angeles education foundation establishes over $12 million education endowment fund supporting youth in Inglewood, California. 2024, August 6. Press release. Accessed March 9, 2025. https://www.prnewswire.com/news-releases/greater-los-angeles-education-foundation-establishes-over-12-million-education-endowment-fund-supporting-youth-in-inglewood-california-302215492.html

LACOE (Los Angeles County Office of Education). n.d. About. Accessed February 24, 2025. https://www.lacoe.edu/about/numbers

LACOE (Los Angeles County Office of Education). 2024. LACOE by the numbers. Accessed February 24, 2025. https://www.lacoe.edu/content/dam/lacoeedu/documents/communications/about-lacoe/lacoe%20by%20the%20numbers.pdf

LAUSD (Los Angeles Unified School District). 2025a. About. Accessed February 24, 2025. https://www.lausd.org/domain/4

NCES (National Center for Educational Statistics). 2022. Enrollment, poverty, and federal funds for the 120 largest school districts, by enrollment size in 2021: School year 2019–20 and fiscal year 2022. Accessed March 9, 2025. https://nces.ed.gov/programs/digest/d22/tables/dt22_215.30.asp

5 Jacksonville Public Education Fund

Jacksonville is located along the St. John's River in Northeast Florida. The city is named after Andrew Jackson, the nation's seventh president, although he never lived there. Commonly referred to by its nickname "Jax," it is the most populous city in Florida and in the southeastern United States, with more than 975,000 residents (World Atlas, 2025). Having merged with a significant portion of Duval County, in which it is located, it is also among the largest cities in the United States by land mass. It is a major deep water port and has a significant military presence, including two naval air stations. With twenty-two miles of beaches, Jacksonville is a tourist destination as well as a center for industry and shipping (Britannica, 2025).

Serving the City of Jacksonville and the county, the Duval County Public Schools is the 18th largest district in the nation, enrolling more than 130,000 students in 197 schools, including forty-four public charter schools (DCPS, 2025). More than 20 percent of students are from backgrounds defined as poverty (DCES, 2023). The district is governed by an elected school board, which appoints the superintendent. At the time of this writing, the superintendent was Dr. Christopher Bernier, appointed in 2024.

Jacksonville Public Education Fund History and Overview

The Jacksonville Public Education Fund (JPEF) was founded in 2009, tracing its history to a foundation created in the 1980s, which focused mostly on teacher recognition. That foundation was restructured in 2000, to primarily focus on efficient operation of the district and develop a board of business leaders who offered certain programs. In 2004, concerns about school performance gained attention and The Community Foundation for Northeast Florida created a Forum on Quality Education, which brought community leaders together to discuss solutions to problems. Their discussions identified the need for a permanent organization to secure private funds for the schools that eventually led to the creation of JPEF (JPEF, 2025a). As the Fund's current president explains, "the vision was to create an independent, high capacity local education fund, meaning research-based, community engaged, and having competency spanning policy and practice" (Fortune, 2025a). The Fund defines itself as "an independent think-and-do tank that believes in the potential of all students. We convene educators, school system leaders, and the community to pilot and help scale evidence-based solutions that advance school quality in Duval County" (JPEF, 2025b). Since its founding, the Fund has facilitated more than $37.5 million in support to the school district, including through fiscal agency, Quality Education for All investments, and investments through JPEF programming (Fortune, 2025b).

Rachael Tutwiler Fortune was appointed as president of The Jacksonville Public Education Fund in 2018. Having begun her career in education as a Teach for America member teaching in Duval County, Fortune subsequently became a program manager at JPEF. She went on to serve in other leadership positions in the field of education, including as a program officer in the Office of the Deputy Secretary of the United States Department of Education during the Obama administration, before returning to JPEF as executive vice president in 2017, transitioning to president in 2018 (JPEF 2025c). The Fund has a full-time staff of fifteen including a vice president who manages program operations and a fund development director (Fortune, 2025a).

The Fund is independent of the school district and is located in separate facilities. Rachael Fortune (2025a) explains that the founders envisioned the Fund serving as a "critical friend" to the school district; however, the relationship has evolved to be a collaboration, "built on a foundation of trust and transparency." In addition to constant communication, to maximize impact and build relationships, she meets formally with the superintendent as well as with her chief of staff monthly. Fortune (2025a) refers to this as "alignment," which ultimately ensures there is a "return on investment" in delivering results for students.

The JPEF operates within an established "strategic framework," which she describes as "intentionally nimble," allowing for adaptation as annual operating plans are developed. A new strategic planning process was about to unfold when Fortune spoke with the authors in 2025. The 2024–6 strategic framework encompasses three mission goals as well as an operational goal. The mission goals include serving as a "research-driven organization and as a respected voice in our community on educational issues." Fortune (2025a) explains, "The Fund works to provide fresh insights and an independent perspective on various issues." Second, the mission also aims to assure that "educators are inspired, motivated, and supported to advance sustained excellence in schools." Initiatives related to this goal include serving as a convener, offering targeted professional learning opportunities, and direct support for teachers and school administrators. Third, the Fund seeks to "identify common priorities or areas in which we want to have an impact and bring diverse stakeholders to the same table to talk about how we can support improvement" (Fortune, 2025a). The JPEF's operational goal, related to all three of the mission goals, is to operate as an efficient and sustainable organization.

In addition to managing its own programs, the Fund serves as a fiscal agent, accepting and managing money on behalf of the school district, school programs, and other organizations supporting schools that have yet to achieve their tax-exempt nonprofit status.

Governance and Board Role

The JPEF's board operates under bylaws that provide for a minimum of thirteen and a maximum of nineteen members, who generally may serve up to two consecutive four-year terms. The superintendent and the chair of the school board serve as ex-officio members, without a vote, as does the Teacher of the Year during the period in which they hold that designation. At the time of her conversation with the authors in 2025, Rachael Fortune indicated that the Fund was looking at alternative approaches, including a study of peer organizations in Florida and across the country, some of which have the superintendent of schools as a voting member of their boards.

Fortune emphasizes the deliberate consideration given to selecting new board members, a process managed by the governance committee. Criteria for the selection include broad representation of the Jacksonville community as well as relevant experience and expertise. The responsibilities and expectations of board members are outlined in a formal document and include serving on at least one committee and providing financial support, either personally or through a company, at a level that makes the fund "one of their top charities of choice" (Fortune, 2025a).

Fundraising and Philanthropy

In 2023, the Fund's total revenue was more than $2.3 million, including more than $2 million in contributions and grants (JPEF, 2023a). The largest source of revenue for the Fund is foundations, accounting for 45 percent. Individual donors, corporations, and the city account for about 7 percent each and the balance comes from various other sources (Fortune, 2025a). Efforts to further diversify revenue sources is a goal for JPEF's fundraising initiatives include an emphasis on cultivating new relationships with individuals and new companies located in Jacksonville.

Fundraising is primarily staff-led and accounts for a substantial portion of the president's time. Board members also are engaged in cases where their relationships may be helpful. Fundraising methods include proposal-writing as well as the use of traditional direct mail, digital giving campaigns, and a biennial luncheon, known as, "EDTalks." The EDTalks event features a well-known speaker who addresses current topics related to education. The Fund views it as an opportunity to enlist donors and also to raise community awareness about important issues and the current thinking of well-recognized experts.

Donors to JPEF are recognized as members of the BEAMS Giving Society, in levels according to the amount of their gift. Members of the highest level, Bridge Builders give $10,000 or more annually or $834 per month. They are recognized in the Fund's annual report and receive a monthly report on the Fund's impact (JPEF, 2025d).

Programs and Impact

The Fund's various programs and initiatives are identified according to their impact on constituencies, including "for educators, "for parents," and "for students." A summary compiled from the Fund's website is included in Box 5.1. With regard to current and emerging priorities, Rachael Fortune identifies four areas. First, the need to recruit, support, and retain talent, including teachers and school staff. As she explains, "We're not a recruitment organization, but we provide support to the district through our programmatic initiatives." She identifies special needs educators as a current priority, given a shortage of professionals in that field. A second area of emphasis is literacy, with math capability growing in importance. A third priority relates to providing students with "holistic support," including initiatives to sustain their overall wellness. The fourth area of growing emphasis is preparing students for success in an environment driven by rapid technological change (Fortune, 2025a).

Fortune views it as essential to prepare students to understand and utilize new technology, such as artificial intelligence, and also to help teachers understand and address the future of learning, so that they "can be prepared for their careers in this evolving digital landscape" (2025a). The Fund's efforts have included working with the district's career and technical education department and purchasing advanced technology so that teachers can become familiar with its use.

BOX 5.1 Jacksonville Public Education Fund Programs

FOR EDUCATORS

School Leadership Initiative

Inspired by Dr. Shawn Ginwright's seminal work, "The Four Pivots," this program will guide school leaders in adopting healing-centered leadership practices to create safe, supportive, and thriving educational environments.

School leaders participate in professional learning sessions and engage in hands-on activities to learn and implement restorative practices that address the traumas faced by students, teachers, and families.

Teacher Leadership Initiative

TLI is multi-faceted, dynamic, and designed to elevate teachers' support and instruction of students, through engaging in monthly training, annual deeper fellowship work, day-to-day coaching, and excellence recognition through the Teacher of the Year process and other leadership opportunities.

Edelman Fellowship for Excellence in Teaching

This initiative allows educators to select and engage in professional development experiences tailored to their individual career aspirations.

There is a selection process with a select group of educators having the opportunity each year.

Wolfburg Fellowship

The newest iteration of this project has been a Youth Participatory Action Research Project, in which students and teachers in Duval County collectively work to answer a research question and the project is led by students themselves.

Teacher of the Year

Teachers are the number one in-classroom predictor of student success, which is why JPEF recognizes outstanding teachers through the Teacher of the Year (TOY) initiative.

FOR PARENTS

Parents Who Lead

Parents Who Lead prepares [parents] to be more actively involved in child advocacy. The program organizes events for participants to learn about the structure of local government and empowers parents to translate problems into action.

New Worlds Reading Initiative

JPEF is a proud Regional Partner of the New Worlds Reading Initiative, Florida's free at-home literacy program designed to help eligible ... students enhance their literacy skills and cultivate a lifelong love of reading. Each month, eligible children receive a free book tailored to their interests, accompanied by resources and activities for caregivers and children to enjoy together.

Urban Education Summit

JPEF, in partnership with My Village Project and 904WARD, hosts this annual event to advance progress and innovation in urban education. The event brings together educators, students, parents, community advocates, and nonprofit organizations collaborating with schools.

FOR STUDENTS

While students are at the center of all the work that JPEF does when supporting educators, engaging parents, and policy makers, JPEF also provides unique opportunities for students to lead themselves in research and advocacy. Example opportunities from 2024 include:

- Youth Participatory Action Research for the Wolfburg Fund for Social Justice
- School Board Voting Videos
- Urban Education Symposium sessions

SOURCE: JPEF (Jacksonville Public Education Fund). 2025. Our work. Accessed April 9, 2025. https://www.jaxpef.org/our-work/. Adapted by the authors from the JPEF website, with additions from JPEF (Rachael Tutwiler Fortune, email to authors, April 30, 2025.) Used with permission.

In addition to managing programs, JPEF engages in advocacy to raise awareness, share viewpoints, and build consensus on education issues. Its Advocacy Center tracks relevant legislation, provides advice on how citizens can contact their legislators, and offers educational materials on the legislative process. Its website provides a link enabling citizens to identify and contact their elected state representatives (JPEF, 2025e).

The JPEF has engaged directly on certain issues and legislation that impacts education. As an example, Rachael Fortune mentions, "We had a sales tax referendum that passed in 2020 and a property tax referendum that passed in 2022." The Fund had taken a position favoring those referenda because of their importance to funding for public education. Fortune (2025a) explains that JPEF has "a process by which we make decisions as an organization as to whether we will use our organizational voice on any particular issue." The process includes specific criteria that have been approved by the Fund's board, including mission alignment, the Fund's expertise on the issue, and consideration of other relationships, and collaborations (Fortune, 2025a).

In Fortune's (2025a) words, the Fund's advocacy is not always "capital A advocacy." In some instances, it involves JPEF providing research on the question and collaborating with other groups. As an example, the Fund partners with the Duval County Public Schools and Kids Hope Alliance to prepare parents for advocacy action. Fortune (2025a) mentions that collaboration is intended "to build the civic leadership skills of parents, who may already be engaged in their PTAs or their school advisory committee, but who are really looking to take their leadership to new heights, to be not just be a champion for their own child, but for all children." She observes, "Having those parents lead other parents is a beautiful thing to witness."

Fortune (2025a) believes that keeping the emphasis on students is an effective way to bridge competing views on education, but she also notes the broader need to develop skills for bringing people together — "I think if we seek to understand each other, then we need to remove preconceived notions." She adds, "I'd love to get back to just those foundational skills of how we interact with each other to move some of these conversations and actions forward on behalf of students" (Fortune, 2025a).

The Fund evaluates the impact of its programs and initiatives using a variety of measures. A recent annual report describes legislative achievements, research reports delivered, survey data from principals and teachers on the impact of specific programs, data on reduced school vacancies, and progress toward the objectives included in its 2024–26 strategic framework (JPEF, 2023b).

Trends and Challenges

When asked to identify challenges faced by the JPEF, Fortune mentions the challenge of communicating about its work and the issues it addresses in a changing media environment. For example, while the Fund does post complete research study reports on its website, it also has recognized the need to package information in ways that will capture attention that includes more use of infographics, short videos, and other formats. Fortune (2025a) explains, "we need to make sure that we are meeting people where they are."

Fortune (2025a) also calls for collaborative leadership and active listening as another tool for effective communication. Fortune (2025a) refers to the changing environment as having a "politically charged nature." Even so, while this environment creates challenges, Fortune (2025a) focuses on opportunities for sharing, saying that "we must understand the perspectives of others and really have an openness to leaning into the historical lens and lived experiences" (Fortune, 2025a).

As a broader challenge, Fortune cites trends affecting public education. They include the decline in students' academic performance, especially since 2020, and diminishing consensus about public policy. She notes that there once seemed to be a mutual understanding regarding public education, but the topic now has become politically sensitive.

Fortune (2025a) observes that "during my earlier stint at JPEF, I led our community engagement work and it was very much about bringing different parts of Jacksonville around the table together, crafting a vision for the future." Even in more divisive times, she views the Fund's role as trying to develop consensus. One strategy is to "make sure that students remain at the center of the conversation." However, she acknowledges the existence of deeper problems in the current state of public dialog, observing that "the skill that seems to be missing in so much of how we interact with each other these days is active listening, really being able to more deeply understand the perspective of another person."

In reflecting on the future of public school education foundations generally, Fortune (2025a) expresses the hope that foundations may be able to increase their financial support to benefit school districts and students. But she also returns to the overriding need for foundations to serve as a "bridge, working to bring key parties together." "I think there's a huge leadership role for foundations to play in making sure that students remain at the center of the dialog."

References

Britannica. 2025. Jacksonville. Accessed April 9, 2025. https://www.britannica.com/place/Jacksonville-Florida

NCES (National Center for Education Statistics). 2023. Enrollment, poverty, and federal funds for the 120 largest school districts, by enrollment size in 2021: School year 2019–20 and fiscal year 2022. Accessed December 12, 2023. https://nces.ed.gov/programs/digest/d22/tables/dt22_215.30.asp

DCPS (Duval County Public Schools). 2025. About. https://www.duvalschools.org/o/dcps/page/about-dcps

Fortune, Rachael Tutwiler. 2025a. Interview with authors, April 23, 2025.

Fortune, Rachael Tutwiler, 2025b. Email to authors, April 30, 2025.

JPEF (Jacksonville Public Education Fund). 2023a. Form 990. Accessed April 24, 2025. https://projects.propublica.org/nonprofits/organizations/592756660/202400999349301800/full

JPEF (Jacksonville Public Education Fund). 2023b. 2022–2023 impact report. Accessed April 24, 2025. https://www.jaxpef.org/media/1ieat3fu/2022-2023-annual-report_jpef_final-1.pdf

JPEF (Jacksonville Public Education Fund). 2025a. History. Accessed April 9, 2025. https://www.jaxpef.org/about-us/history/

JPEF (Jacksonville Public Education Fund). 2025b. Our work. Accessed April 23, 2025. https://www.jaxpef.org/our-work/

JPEF (Jacksonville Public Education Fund). 2025c. About us. Accessed April 9, 2025. https://www.jaxpef.org/about-us/staff-directory/rachael-tutwiler-fortune/

JPEF (Jacksonville Public Education Fund). 2025d. Building the bridge. Accessed April 24, 2025. https://www.jaxpef.org/get-involved/beams-giving-society/

JPEF (Jacksonville Public Education Fund). 2025e. Advocacy center. Accessed April 23, 2025. https://www.jaxpef.org/advocacy-center/

World Atlas. 2025. 10 largest cities in Florida. Accessed April 9, 2025. https://www.worldatlas.com/cities/10-largest-cities-in-florida.html

6 Denver Public Schools Foundation

Known as the "Mile High City" because of its elevation, Denver is the capital of Colorado and the most populous city in the state. Named in 1858 after James W. Denver, the governor of the Kansas Territory that then encompassed the city, Denver today is the center of a metropolitan area that is a center for transportation, a thriving nonprofit sector, high-technology industry, and education, including the University of Denver. The main campus of the University of Colorado is located in nearby Boulder (Britannica, 2025).

The Denver Public Schools (DPS), serving both the city and county of Denver, is governed by a board of education including seven members, five of whom are elected within regions and two of whom are elected at-large across the city. The board appoints the superintendent of schools, who at the time of this writing was Dr. Alex Marrero. The district encompasses 207 schools, enrolling more than 90,000 students, including 36 percent who are Spanish-speaking (DPS, 2025). The DPS has faced challenges in recent years, including declining overall enrollment as well as an influx of new arrivals, requiring increased resources for multilingual education and other services (DPS, 2024).

Denver Public Schools Foundation History and Overview

The Denver Public Schools Foundation (DPS Foundation) was established in 1992 and in its early years it focused on classroom grants. Beginning in the 2000s, its mission broadened to encompass support for district-wide priorities. The initiative to expand the Foundation came from the then-superintendent, Michael Bennet, now a United States Senator, and a group of local citizens, who provided personal gifts. A capacity-building grant from a local foundation enabled the Foundation to expand its mission (DPSF, n.d.; Hazel, 2025). By 2023, the Foundation's revenue had grown to more than $7 million and it awarded grants totaling almost $7 million (DPSF, 2023). The DPS Foundation supports both traditional public schools and charter schools, which, in Colorado, are part of the school district. There are other nonprofit organizations that also support Denver Public Schools in more specialized ways, for example, the Denver Scholarship Foundation (DSF), which provides support to help public school graduates attend college and explore career opportunities (DSF, 2025).

Sara Hazel joined the DPS Foundation in 2020 as vice president for development and impact, following twenty years serving in fundraising positions at well-known nonprofit organizations, including the American Red Cross, the American Cancer Society, and Girls Inc. of Metro Denver. She became interim CEO in 2021 and was appointed as president and chief executive officer in 2024. As she explains, the transition from the broader nonprofit sector to an education foundation required a "crash course in education" (Hazel, 2025).

As Hazel describes, the DPS Foundation is a "fundraising organization" and its full-time staff of twelve includes a vice president for development, vice president of marketing and communications, and a director of development, directors focused on foundation relations, corporate relations, annual giving, and other related responsibilities. In addition to staff, the Foundation sometimes engages specialized contractors in areas such as marketing, communications, and graphic design.

The DPS Foundation is independent of the school district, but is housed in the district's headquarters facility with a lease agreement. The favorable lease agreement provides the Foundation with an economic advantage and the location places it near day-to-day school district operations.

Hazel (2025) describes the Foundation's relationship with the school district as "ideal," blending independence with close involvement, helping her to stay in touch with the district's priorities. She notes, "I don't report to the superintendent and I don't report to the board of education. I think that gives us a lot more flexibility than if we were part of the district" (Hazel 2025). However, she meets monthly with the superintendent as well as other senior district officials, including the chief financial officer, the deputy superintendent of academics, and the director of strategy. Along with these officials and others, she is a member of the superintendent's leadership team, which meets weekly. She explains, "this helps me define what our foundation priorities need to be, because I am hearing the district's priorities firsthand from the entire leadership team" (2025). Hazel also meets with the school board annually to provide an update on the Foundation's activities. She describes that relationship as positive, saying, "We're doing really good work at the foundation. We have very positive stories to tell and I think they are grateful for our efforts" (Hazel, 2025).

The Foundation has had strategic plans in the past, usually aligned with the district's strategic plan, but Hazel is now taking a more flexible approach. As of the date of Hazel's conversation with the authors in 2025, the Foundation was engaged in developing a "strategic framework" to identify forces "globally and nationally that will impact our work." Hazel emphasized that the purpose was to maintain flexibility and not produce "a piece of paper that's thrown in a desk drawer." She explained, "I don't want a strategic plan that tells me where we are going to be in three to five years," further adding, "I want a plan that helps us identify the *questions* we will need to be asking in order to make decisions in the next three to five years" (Hazel, 2025).

Governance and Board Role

According to its bylaws, the Foundation's board includes fifteen to thirty members, who serve three-year terms, renewable to a maximum of nine years. As of the time of this writing, the board had twenty-five members, including corporate and nonprofit executives and the provost of the University of Denver. The Foundation's CEO, the superintendent of schools, and the chair of the school board serve as ex-officio members. Board committees include an executive committee and committees focused on governance, finance, marketing and communications, and grantmaking.

Given the DPS Foundation's emphasis on fundraising, board members are expected to give-or-get a minimum annual gift of $20,000. Since many are corporate officials, these gifts are often made by their companies, although the board positions are not "company seats" (Hazel, 2025). Board members also become involved in fundraising by helping to make connections with other individual and corporate donors. Given the Foundation's experienced fundraising staff, they generally are not required to become involved in actual solicitations, although they do help to make introductions and build relationships with prospective donors.

In addition to the ability to make or bring a gift, criteria for board-membership include a passion for public education and the Denver schools. If they are DPS parents or alumni, that is "all the better" (Hazel, 2025). Directors are selected in terms of experiences and skills related to the foundation's work, including finance, investments, and expertise on education matters. Diversity is an important criterion, in order to assure that the board reflects the community (Hazel, 2025).

The board is actively involved and the staff works to keep them informed. However, as Hazel (2025) notes, the DPS Foundation's staff is relatively large compared to many education foundations and is able to handle the hands-on work, with input and advice from the board.

Fundraising and Philanthropy

As mentioned previously, fundraising is a primary activity of the Foundation and its staff includes fundraising professionals. As of 2025, 57 percent of the revenue was derived from independent foundations, 12 percent from individual donors, 11 percent from investment income, 8 percent from events, 5 percent from corporations and corporate foundations, 5 percent from gifts-in-kind, and the balance from other sources (Hazel, 2025). Hazel observes that private foundations are often the largest source of support for public school foundations, since many have education as a programmatic focus.

School district leaders are not directly involved in fundraising. However, the Foundation is an "active listener" in the district's discussions and identifies gaps to discuss with potential funders (Hazel, 2025) which often requires "a marriage between philanthropic interests and what the district wants" (Hazel, 2025). Not every need identified by the district may be attractive to a donor and not every donor interest is consistent with the district's priorities, so the Foundation is required to look for overlapping priorities.

The Foundation's fundraising activities include writing grant proposals, in partnership with DPS, and managing two fundraising events annually. Those include the Achieve Gala and the Back to Class Bash, which engages community and corporate volunteers in school projects. The Foundation also utilizes direct mail and other methods to solicit gifts and participates in the Colorado Gives Day every December, which has proven to be an effective source of individual gifts (Hazel, 2025). The most successful fundraising involves personal relationships, which involve "building trust and accountability and finding people who care about equity and education" (Hazel, 2025). Contacts with donors and relationship-building activities occupy a significant portion of the CEO's time. A development committee, which includes some members of the board of directors as well as other individuals, helps to make introductions and host events that engage potential new donors.

Future fundraising will place an increased emphasis on planned giving, encompassing gifts that involve donors' financial and estate plans, with the goal of increasing the Foundation's endowment. As of 2025, the DPS Foundation had two endowed funds, one unrestricted and another restricted to making grants to teachers. Sara Hazel (2025) states, "My dream scenario is that we have a major endowment campaign where we raise enough that we can be less focused on unrestricted money to operate and just focus on directing more money to supporting our students, families, and educators." She also recognizes the need for "creative philanthropy" and for developing models that bring alternative sources of revenue to the district. One example she offered as creative philanthropy is working with developers and property owners to offer free or low-cost housing for teachers, a topic that is discussed further below.

Programs and Impact

The DPS Foundation defines its activities in four broad areas according to impact: students, educators, families, and emerging needs. Box 6.1, based on the DPS Foundation website at the time of this writing, summarizes its programs in these areas.

Box 6.1 Denver Public Schools Foundation Programs and Initiatives

Students

Afterschool Programs
A place for students to feel safe, have fun, and engage in enriching educational activities.

Career and College Success

We're strengthening the pipeline to success through Career and College Success (CCS).

Middle School Sports

The DPS Foundation funds Prep League, a competitive sports league for 6th–8th graders.

Exceptional Student Services

Ensuring that all students can access and engage in learning, and experience belonging in their school communities.

Student Grantmaking

Returning power to DPS students through direct funding for their ideas and projects.

Educators

A to Z Fund

Provides materials, resources and opportunities that fall outside classroom budgets.

Housing

We have partnered with Grand Peaks to offer one year of rent-free housing to 10 Denver Public Schools (DPS) educators.

Educators Take Flight

Provides the opportunity for DPS educators to travel for learning opportunities.

Families

New Arrivals, Student & Family Fund

A relief fund that provided support for new-to-country families in DPS.

Community Hubs

Wrap-around services for students, families and our community.

Emerging Needs

Connection and Independence
Unlike other entities, we have a direct connection to the district while also maintaining our own independent status. This means we are not bound by typical funding constraints or strict budgets. As a result, we possess the flexibility to swiftly respond to emerging needs as they arise. One way we responded swiftly was through our New Arrivals: Student & Family Fund.

Proactive Approach
When challenges arise that can be addressed through funding, we are poised to act immediately. Our ability to allocate resources, collaborate with various stakeholders, and explore innovative solutions enables us to effectively support students, educators, and schools. This proactive approach ensures that we can foster a more resilient and successful educational environment.

SOURCE: DPSF (Denver Public Schools Foundation). 2025. What we support. Accessed April 10, 2025. https://dpsfoundation.org/what-we-support/students/. Adapted by the authors. Used with permission

In 2025, Sara Hazel explained that support for students, educators, and families are core priorities and the needs are only growing. The Foundation provided emergency support during the COVID-19 pandemic, creating a fundraising campaign to provide food when schools were out of session. In 2024 and 2025, Denver received thousands of new arrivals from other countries, which increased needs in the community and schools. The DPS Foundation created a New Arrivals Fund that helped schools obtain furniture and equipment needed to serve the new students as well as tools such as translation tablets. While the Foundation continues to support families, Hazel observes that there also are other community organizations that do so. In some cases, the DPS Foundation serves as a "connector" that helps families access needed assistance from those sources. Another area of focus includes after-school programs. As Hazel notes, such programs benefit the students and parents, who may be better able to accommodate their own workplace demands as a result. While there are other organizations that serve the community, students, and families, there are fewer organizations that support teachers. "Helping recruit and retain high quality educators and providing them with the resources and support they need" is thus a particular emphasis for the Denver Public Schools Foundation (Hazel, 2025).

An area of particular and growing interest to Sara Hazel is housing for teachers. She notes that Denver and some nearby communities have relatively high housing costs which makes the teachers who live far away face long commutes. That may make it difficult to attract and retain teachers as well as draining their own energies. The Foundation has partnered with real estate company Grand Peaks to provide free rent for some teachers in Denver. Hazel (2025) explains, "How this started was the private sector coming to us. It was a developer saying, 'We are opening a 700 unit apartment complex and we want to do something good for the community. We'd like to give 10 teachers free housing for a year.'" Hazel (2025) acknowledges a need to evaluate the impact of this initiative, saying "Let's see how this impacts the performance of those teachers, whether they stay in the district, and look at other measures." She considers the partnership with Grand Peaks to be a pilot and views teacher housing as an area in which the Foundation may continue to focus, exploring additional opportunities to increase affordability and perhaps also create a revenue stream for the Foundation. In addition, Hazel (2025) is exploring options with the school district to utilize vacant school buildings for potential revenue generation, perhaps as a location for nonprofits and small businesses to utilize office space and shared services.

Affordable housing is a problem in many school districts in high-cost areas, some of which have built housing on their own land for leasing to teachers. This is not a model that Hazel thinks would work in Denver, but she plans to continue exploring options through the DPS Foundation and thinks that housing may become a higher priority for other public school foundations as well.

The Denver Public Schools Foundation has not been engaged in advocacy for most of its history, but its board did publicly support a bond issue on the ballot in 2024. Hazel believes the Foundation may become more active in the policy area in the future and returns to the importance of providing affordable teacher housing. "Something I've been pondering for a while now," she says, "is whether there could be policies that encourage landlords to rent at a discount to a teacher in exchange for a tax credit and still make whatever they need to make" (Hazel, 2025).

The Foundation evaluates and communicates the impact of its programs. Its staff includes a person dedicated to this effort, whose role is to evaluate the impact of the Foundation's grants. In addition, on some occasions the Foundation has engaged outside contractors to help evaluate data and develop tools to track and share impact. It also publishes a quarterly "impact report" (Hazel, 2025). She further observes that obtaining outcome data regarding students has become more challenging in recent times, as a result of policies regarding privacy. She views this reality as perhaps a downside of being an independent organization outside of the district's control. She also is realistic about the ability to attribute impact, explaining, "For example, we may have used funds to build a community garden at a school. That may bring important benefits, but I'm certainly not able to argue that it allowed a student to graduate from high school on time ten years later."

Trends and Challenges

Sara Hazel (2025) sees opportunities as well as challenges for the DPS Foundation. As she explains, Colorado has an unusual funding model for public education, which limits support. "We have what's called the Colorado Paradox," she says, "meaning that we have a highly educated workforce, but our schools are not well-funded. We're not growing our own." That reality is a challenge for the DPS Foundation, which cannot totally meet the district's growing needs and must focus on its core purposes. One avenue the Foundation is exploring includes more collaboration with other nonprofits interested in schools in the area. As an example, in 2023, it brought together other foundations and groups concerned with school safety, an experience that may provide a model for approaching other issues. "The role of convener is one I think we can fill," says Hazel. While the DPS Foundation has not played the role of fiscal sponsor in the past, Hazel envisions the possibility of increased collaborative funding in future years, perhaps involving the foundation and other nonprofit partners (Hazel, 2025).

In looking at the universe of public school education foundations, Hazel (2025) sees challenges in the increased politicization of discussions about public education in many areas, which complicates discussions with donors. Nevertheless, she anticipates increasing growth—"I think public school foundations will be important as we lose public funding for education. School districts that do not have them are creating them." She suggests that meeting the need will require that school foundations become more professionalized and effective at fundraising, becoming more like institutionally-related foundations in higher education. The DPS has many successful alumni and there is wealth in the community, so the potential for increased giving exists. But Hazel sees a need for better messaging, making the case for support at the district level and addressing the reality that many individuals care more about their individual schools than the district overall. She states, "K-12 education is formative, just like college, and we need people to feel that DPS is an amazing place to have on their resume. That means that *all* of our schools must be really good." "It's an amazing time to be in a public education foundation," she adds, "because we have the opportunity to do really, really good things in tough times."

References

Britannica. 2025. Denver. Accessed April 10, 2025. https://www.britannica.com/place/Denver

DPS (Denver Public Schools). 2024. State of the district update. Accessed May 2, 2025. https://www.dpsk12.org/article/1454588

DPS (Denver Public Schools). 2025. Website. Accessed April 10, 2025. https://www.dpsk12.org/

DPSF (Denver Public Schools Foundation). n.d. 30 stories for 30 years. Accessed May 1, 2025. https://dpsfoundation.org/wp-content/uploads/2024/10/DPSF_AR22_FINAL2_web.pdf

DPSF (Denver Public Schools Foundation). 2023. Form 990. Accessed May 1, 2025. https://projects.propublica.org/nonprofits/organizations/841224325/202443259349301759/full

DSF (Denver Scholarship Foundation). 2025. Website. Accessed May 1, 2025. https://denverscholarship.org/

Hazel, Sara. 2025. Interview with authors, May 1, 2025.

7 Austin Ed Fund

Named after Stephen F. Austin, known as the "Father of Texas," the city of Austin is the capital of the state of Texas. The city was founded in the 1830s, while the area was still a part of Mexico. The Greater Austin area is home to the main campus of the University of Texas and to many prominent corporations, including Dell Technologies and Tesla. Known for its active music and arts scene, it is the home of the annual South by Southwest Conference, which focuses on music, film, and interactive media and attracts international attendees (Visit Austin, 2025).

The Austin Independent School District (AISD) serves the city of Austin and includes 116 schools enrolling more than 73,000 students of diverse backgrounds. Of its total student population, more than 50 percent are classified as economically disadvantaged (AISD, 2025). The district is governed by an elected, nine-member board of trustees, which appoints the school superintendent, who was Matias Segura at the time of writing this book.

Austin Ed Fund History and Overview

The Austin Ed Fund (AEF) was established as the Austin Public Education Foundation in 1993 and since 2001, it has facilitated more than $51 million in support of the school system, students, and teachers. In 2015, the Fund launched a grant program that by 2025 had awarded more than $2.1 million to support more than 400 teacher-driven projects with a focus on innovative classroom practices and educational opportunities for economically disadvantaged students. In addition to its own grants, the Fund supports district-wide initiatives and encourages the community to make gifts to support teachers, students, and school district programs (AISD, 2025).

Michelle Wallis was appointed as the Fund's executive director in 2012. With a background in social work, Wallis previously had served as the executive director of the Ann Richards School Foundation and in other nonprofit organizations, including United Way (Wallis, 2025a). She explains that the move from working with an individual school to the district level was attractive given the "opportunity to have a larger impact on education" (Wallis, 2025a).

The Fund experienced distinct periods in its history, including varied roles and relationships with the school district. During certain periods it has served as essentially "a kitchen cabinet" for the superintendent, providing a trusted space to think through ideas, opportunities, and challenges. During other periods, its role was exclusively that of a fiscal agent, not engaging in active fundraising but providing a vehicle for donors who wanted to support a program within the school system. And there were periods in which it was essentially dormant. Today it is highly active and embedded in the school district, working to advance the district's priorities (Wallis, 2025a).

Wallis serves in a dual role as executive director of AISD's Office of Innovation and Development (OID), reporting to the superintendent, as well as executive director of the AEF, reporting to its board. The work of OID and AEF are closely related. The OID is charged with strategic design and innovation and resource development to provide opportunities for AISD students. The AEF is the office's nonprofit partner in those activities and secures private support to fund initiatives. Given her dual role, Wallis interacts frequently with the superintendent and other school district officials regarding their priorities. Staff support for the AEF is provided by OID, with a memorandum of understanding that defines arrangements for the sharing of resources and costs between the district and the Fund (Wallis, 2025a).

In addition to its own fundraising and grant programs, the Fund provides technical support and training to school district personnel with regard to proposal writing and maintains partnerships with crowdfunding platforms Follett Destiny Fundraising Manager and Donors Choose, used for fundraising by campuses, teachers, and PTAs (Wallis, 2025a).

Wallis's approach to leadership of AEF is strategy-driven. The Fund developed a strategic plan for 2024–7 that focuses on three priorities: Grow Impact, Build Champions, and Increase Organizational Excellence. The plan defines the Fund's mission as "[inspiring] the community to invest in Austin ISD" and identifies goals and objectives for each of the three priorities (Wallis, 2025b).

Governance and Board Role

The AEF board included twenty-nine individuals at the time of this writing. Two school district officials, the superintendent and the chair of the district's board of trustees, serve as ex-officio members of the AEF board, with a vote. Other board members include leaders drawn from businesses and nonprofit organizations in Austin (AEF, 2025; Wallis, 2025a).

The AEF board is governed by formal bylaws that prescribe an executive committee and committees focused on nominations, governance, grant-review, finance, and audit. Another board committee specifically supports the annual Inspire the Future Luncheon, a major fundraising initiative of the Fund (Wallis, 2025a). Board members serve a maximum of two three-year terms and complete an annual board member agreement based on an established job description. The governance committee manages the process of recruiting board members, with the goal of assuring that membership reflects the Austin community and its industries.

Board members are expected to attend and participate in meetings and other events and provide financial support to the Fund at "a personally significant level" (Wallis, 2025a). Wallis thinks that this approach is likely to result in a larger amount of board support, in contrast with a minimum-gift policy, which may limit some board members' gifts to that amount.

Fundraising and Philanthropy

The AEF received revenue of more than $3.4 million in 2023. Sources included private foundations (69 percent), corporations (1.4 percent), special events (16 percent), individuals (7 percent), and other (6 percent) (AEF, 2023; Wallis, 2025a). Corporate support is growing and the Fund is making increased efforts to obtain support from individual donors.

The Fund's primary fundraising initiative is the annual Inspire the Future Luncheon. The event attracts sponsors, who are listed on the AEF website by the level of their support. The board committee that is focused on the luncheon assists in identifying and soliciting donors and sponsors (Wallis, 2025a). The event also provides a setting for developing relationships with prospective donors. The executive director and the development staff follow up after the event to discuss potential gifts to the Fund. The superintendent attends some meetings with donors, with the purpose of providing information on the district's priorities (Wallis, 2025a).

The Fund's webpage provides the opportunity to make a gift to support a specific campus within the district or for other purposes. Donors of $1,000 or more are recognized as members of the Leadership Giving Circle, at various levels based on gift amount. The Fund's website provides the option to make a one-time gift or pledge monthly contributions (AEF, 2025).

In a conversation with the authors, Michelle Wallis explained that AEF's approach to fundraising has evolved, saying, "In the past, we have been primarily oriented toward responding to RFPs, which of course reflect the priorities of funders. We are now more proactive and focused on raising funds specifically to address school district priorities." She notes that the district has seen budget reductions and while "it is not possible for AEF to make up the shortfall, we can help to plug some holes, maintain the spirit of creativity and innovation, and meet emerging needs" (Wallis, 2025a).

Programs and Impact

The AEF maintains grant programs supporting classroom projects and districtwide initiatives. It also maintains a crisis support fund. The latter was initiated in collaboration with AISD during the COVID-19 pandemic and raised more than $10 million to meet educational and community needs. It has been maintained post-pandemic to address continuing needs, such as access to food services, health programs, and others (Wallis, 2025a). The AEF does not specifically participate in advocacy activities, but it does provide information to its board on the implications of relevant legislation (Wallis, 2025a). Box 7.1 provides a summary list of AEF's programs, provided to the authors by the Fund at the time of this writing (Wallis, 2025c).

Box 7.1 Austin Ed Fund Programs

Inspire the Future Grants

Supports creative, educator-led projects and open to all Austin ISD Educators

Crisis Fund

Basic needs assistance and emergency support for Austin ISD students, staff and families

Focus Areas

Initiatives aligned with district priorities that include a suite of high impact strategies for public-private partnership. SY 2024–2025 Focus Areas:

- Early Literacy
- College and Career Readiness
- Educator Experience

In Focus Areas, the Fund does the following:

- Create time and space for *design and strategic thinking*
- *Identify goals* and build *cases for support* for strategies appropriate for partnership and external support
- Identify and investigate *research questions* to improve outcomes for students
- Support *experiments* to build evidence through an innovation cycle
- *Engage partners* including researchers, public and philanthropic funding sources, industry and community
- *Solicit commitments* including grants and donations to support strategies
- Establish cadence for *reflection and improvement*
- *Steward investments* with program and financial support and monitoring

Sponsored Projects and Program Support

Encourage and support donations to Austin ISD campuses and programs

SOURCE: Michelle Wallis, Executive Director, Austin Ed Fund. 2025c. Email to authors, May 8, 2025. Used with permission.

The AEF's current priorities are defined in three focus areas: early literacy, college and career readiness, and educator experience. Wallis (2025a) notes that math is an area of emerging priority. These priorities are shared with Inspire the Future grant applicants. In 2024, 38 percent of the grants were directed to literacy projects, 34 percent to colleges and career readiness initiatives, and

28 percent to the educator experience. Wallis (2025a) explains that the Fund's college visit initiative in 2024–5 will include more than 110 visits, with more than 7,400 students participating. Selected examples of grants in the focus areas, provided on the Fund's website in 2025, include the following:

- Inspire the Future Grant, Andrews Elementary School, Dyslexia Challenge. This project will support bilingual children in overcoming the difficulties and become readers. Grant $7,000. (Literacy)
- 2024 Inspire the Future Grant, Burnet Middle School, Setting the Stage for Dreams to Become Reality. This project is designed to increase college awareness and readiness skills school-wide. It will incorporate a school-family-community partnership to support and empower families as students progress through middle school, high school and into college and careers. Students will participate in workshops, presentations, and field trips that prepare them for college and a career following their post-secondary education. Grant $10,000. (College and Career Readiness)
- 2024 Inspire the Future Grant, Austin ISD Student Support Services, Nurturing Connection and Belonging with Restorative Practices. This project will establish and maintain bi-monthly restorative practices, opportunities to model and engage in relationship-building activities with adults that can be implemented with students. The project will focus on nurturing connection and belonging within the educator experience. Grant $8,800. (Educator Experience)

(AEF, 2025)

The Fund's focus area work has evolved beyond fundraising and grantmaking to include design and strategic thinking, identifying goals and building the case for support, identifying research questions to help improve outcomes, supporting experimental innovations, engaging partners, soliciting financial commitments, reflecting on results, and stewarding investments through monitoring. Wallis notes that strategic work contributes to fundraising success as well as program effectiveness and sustainability (Wallis, 2025a).

Michelle Wallis (2025a) explains that in past years, when AEF served largely as a fiscal agent to manage external grants in support of AISD, performance measures were often defined by the grantors. Now that the Fund has shifted to a proactive approach in support of district priorities, it works to align more closely with AISD's criteria and methods for evaluating outcomes. It also has increased its communication of outcomes and sharing of what has been learned with partners. Box 7.2 provides an example of an outcomes report provided to the authors by the Fund in 2025.

Box 7.2 Austin Ed Fund Outcomes Report

Early Literacy Focus Area

Beginning in Spring 2024, the Austin Ed Fund has collaborated closely with Austin ISD leadership on strategy to improve Early Literacy outcomes and raised $2.154 million for research-based early literacy instruction. Funds have supported:

- curriculum and instructional alignment
- professional development and coaching
- establishment of Lighthouse Schools
- caregiver engagement
- progress monitoring
- instructional materials

Progress will ultimately be measured by the Austin ISD Scorecard Goal for the percentage of 3rd-grade students reading on grade level. Austin ISD and the Ed Fund are tracking leading indicators including the percentage of students recommended for intervention in 2nd grade and indicators of instructional quality. As a part of its reflection cycle, Austin Ed Fund supports the District's regular progress monitoring efforts and related adjustments to district implementation.

From Winter, 2023 to Winter, 2024, after only a few months of implementation, the number of students identified as recommended for intervention in 2nd grade decreased from 32% to 30%, with significant progress for multiple student groups, including a decrease from 48% to 44% for students identified as economically disadvantaged.

Additionally, in Fall, 2024, Austin ISD was seeing shifts in Early Literacy instruction and areas of opportunity:

- Teachers are using adopted curriculum far more consistently (77% of lessons in fall) than in the spring (45% of lessons), driving rapid instructional growth across schools.

- Foundational skills instruction is much improved across all areas (systematic, explicit, and student practice), growing from 32% of lessons in the spring to 47% of lessons in the fall
- Despite these gains, there remains room for growth with providing consistently explicit skills instruction coupled with effective practice in and out of text, with only 44% of classrooms providing students adequate opportunities for practice.
- In reading/listening comprehension, text quality is significantly stronger than it was in spring.
- Though texts are stronger, comprehension instruction itself has not improved (35% of lessons in spring compared to 36% of lessons in fall), indicating a need for greater focus and support around making meaning of text.

College and Career Readiness Focus Area

Austin Ed Fund's work in this area centers around a suite of programs increasing opportunities for students to build their awareness, knowledge and access to postsecondary success.

Strategies include universal college visits provided at scale 5th, 7th and 10th grade students, adistrict-wide summer internship program.

In SY 2023–24, over 3,000 students participated in a college visit. 89% of students reported that the campus visit helped them understand what college is like. Prior to the visit, 21% of students thought attending college would help them achieve their life goals. After the visit, an additional 66% of students agreed or strongly agreed with this statement. In SY 2024–25, it is projected that over 7,400 students will participate in a college visit.

In SY 2023–24, the Ed Fund piloted Austin ISD's Summer Internship Program with 35 students. In SY 2024–25, over 75 students will participate, gaining knowledge and skills and increasing their sense of belonging in a variety of career pathways.

Other strategies are underway, and the Ed Fund uses a reflection cycle to test and adapt its approach to best meet student needs.

SOURCE: Michelle Wallis, Executive Director, Austin Ed Fund. 2025c. Email to authors, May 8, 2025. Used with permission.

Despite the Fund's proactive approach, Wallis notes that there are still many opportunities to play the fiscal agent role by managing grants that may be initiated by foundation or corporate donors. She observes that this role sometimes can be complicated, since outside funders have their own "wants, desires, and priorities" and that sometimes AEF must say "no" to a grant that does not align with the district's needs and priorities or "readiness factors indicate that the program may have limited success" (2025a). This approach is necessary to direct support to the district's established priorities and assure effectiveness.

Trends and Challenges

In her conversation with the authors, Michelle Wallis (2025a) identified trends and challenges being faced by AEF, including budget reductions that have impacted the district. While acknowledging that the Fund is unable to fully compensate for declining public support, she sees it as helping to provide "stability and innovation in times of stress." She explained that her greatest frustration is being aware of the multiple opportunities that AEF may not be able to address. "There are so many opportunities and so many people who want to help," she explains, adding "this is a big district and our evolving role requires focus and the time and space to fully understand the vision and goals of district leaders."

Wallis sees similar challenges faced by public school education foundations nationwide, amid an evolving narrative on public education. She suggests that foundation executives can help schools develop strategies to address the challenges they face. She notes the expanding role of institutionally-related foundations in public higher education and speculates that "perhaps public school foundations today are where *they* were 20 years ago."

References

AEF (Austin Ed Fund). 2025. Website. Accessed March 28, 2025. https://www.austinedfund.org/

AEF (Austin Ed Fund). 2023. Annual report. Accessed March 29, 2025. https://www.austinedfund.org/wp-content/uploads/2025/02/AEF-Annual-Report-2023-online.pdf

AISD (Austin Independent School District). 2025. About. Accessed February, 2025. https://www.austinisd.org/about-us
Visit Austin. 2025. SXSW 2025: South by Southwest conference & festivals. Accessed February 24, 2025. https://www.austintexas.org/events/sxsw/
Wallis, Michelle. 2025a. Interview with authors, March 28, 2025.
Wallis, Michelle. 2025b. Materials provided to authors in email, March 28, 2025.
Wallis, Michelle. 2025c. Email to authors, May 8, 2025.

8 Indianapolis Public Schools Foundation

Indianapolis is the capital city of Indiana and the largest city in the state, with a population of more than 879,000 (Indianapolis, 2025). Founded in 1821 as the state capital, its name is generally thought to mean "land of the Indians," reflecting its history as the original home of several Native American nations. It became an industrial and transportation center with the growth of railroads in the nineteenth century. Sometimes referred to as "Indy," the city's design is based on the layout of Washington, DC. It is known for its art and culture as well as its emphasis on athletics, exemplifiedby the headquarters of the National Collegiate Athletic Association. It also is well-known for motorsports, represented by the annual Indy 500. Indianapolis is home to several universities, including the University of Indiana Indianapolis and Purdue University Indianapolis.

Indianapolis Public Schools (IPS), the largest system in the state, enrolls more than 30,000 students in more than sixty schools. The district serves a diverse student body, including many from low-income households and 20 percent who are English-language learners. Sixty-five percent of students qualify for free or reduced school meals (Bailey, 2025a). The district is governed by an elected board of school commissioners, which appoints the superintendent. At the time of this writing, the superintendent was Dr. Aleesia Johnson, who has served since 2019 (IPS, 2025).

There are more than sixty charter schools in Indianapolis, under a system that began in 2001, when the city first granted the mayor the power to authorize charters. Innovation Network Schools (INS), established through state legislation in 2014, operate within the school district while maintaining autonomy over academics, staffing, and operations. The INS also benefit from district facilities and shared services (Bailey, 2015b).

Indianapolis Public Schools Foundation History and Overview

The Indianapolis Public Schools Foundation (IPSF) was created in the 1980s by a small group of private citizens, who made gifts to provide modest support for teachers. The foundationwas professionalized at the urging of the superintendent of schools, who saw a need for more impactful fundraising (Bailey, 2025a). The IPSF describes its role in three areas:

- Work in close collaboration with district leadership to ensure funding priorities will result in student success.
- Partner with community leaders, business, and philanthropists who invest in the district's priorities.
- Monitor implementation of funded priorities and ensure that all donated funds are managed with integrity. (IPSF, 2025)

The IPSF is the only foundation raising funds for IPS and primarily supporting district-managed schools. It has a close relationship with the leadership of IPS and is housed in the district's offices, despite it being an independent nonprofit organization. Its chief executive officer reports to the foundation's board of directors. It also has a partnership with twenty independent charter schools that are part of the innovation network, described previously. Those schools have their own governing boards and raise funds independently. The IPSF does not raise funds for those schools directly, they are eligible to apply for certain grants from IPSF (Bailey, 2025b).

Having previously held positions in business and nonprofit organizations, Stephannie Bailey was recruited as chief executive officer of the foundation in 2018. Bailey acknowledges that she did not have experience as a career fundraiser, but brought perspectives from her years of nonprofit executive leadership and a background in sales and marketing. In this context, she explains, "What I like to do is find organizations that are not performing to their potential and them help them to exceed expectations" (Bailey, 2025a). Bailey recalls that when she arrived at the Foundation, with the charge of expanding philanthropy, some individuals in the school district were skeptical if such support could be achieved and have a meaningful impact. She states, "We spent a lot of time talking with people about the potential and casting a vision for how significant philanthropy could transform student access, opportunity and outcomes" (Bailey, 2025a). By 2023, the Foundation's annual revenue was more than $5.5 million and it awarded grants of more than $4.5 million (IPSF Form 990).

Bailey directs a full-time staff of five, including a chief operations officer and a chief growth officer, who is responsible for grant development. The Foundation also engages external contractors for services that include financial and database management (Bailey, 2025a).

The IPSF does not manage programs directly and raises funds only for the school district's programs. As the Foundation's CEO, Bailey meets monthly with the district's key leadership and twice a year with the school board, in addition to informal communications on almost a daily basis. Explaining the relationship she says, "our team is expected to have deep knowledge of the district's strategic initiatives and our commitment to the superintendent is that we will never raise a dollar that isn't aligned with the district's priorities" (Bailey, 2025a). What she calls the Foundation's "value proposition" to the district is that "we allow them to stay focused on being the subject matter experts and driving academic outcomes while we stay focused on being their internal philanthropic experts" (Bailey, 2025a).

Governance and Board Role

The IPSF is governed by a self-perpetuating board of directors, which in 2025 included nine members. Board members serve three-year terms for a maximum of nine years. Officers are elected to one-year terms and can serve in those roles up to three years. The superintendent and the board of school commissioners (school board) each appoint one member to the Foundation's board. The appointed members serve with a "voice" rather than a vote. The board once had committees, but the experience was mixed and it was determined that the relatively small size of the board did not justify the volunteer and staff time required to operate them. The only remaining committee is a four-member executive committee (Bailey, 2025a). If a group of board members is needed to focus on a particular question or project, that particular requirement is addressed by creating a temporary task force. The board provides strategic advice to the Foundation and the CEO regarding the overall work of the organization. Board members do not have a specific "give or get" fundraising expectation, but rather are asked to contribute in a meaningful way and support the staff's fundraising by sharing their personal networks and making strategic connections (Bailey, 2025a). Bailey mentions as examples some board members who are corporate executives and help to establish relationships with their corporate foundations or giving programs.

Fundraising and Philanthropy

The IPSF's fundraising is oriented toward securing grants. In 2024, revenue was derived 80 percent from foundations, 17 percent from corporations, 2 percent from individual donors, and the balance form other sources (Bailey, 2025a). The Foundation's funders are a blend of local, regional, and national grantors with a focus on public education. Although the Foundation is limited to accepting private funds, it also plays the role of an "inside consulting firm" (Bailey, 2025a), advising the school district on its applications for state and federal funds. As Bailey (2025a) explains, the Foundation's experience in positioning the district for private grants can also be helpful in crafting proposals for public funding opportunities.

The Foundation's plans for increasing philanthropic support include a continued emphasis on foundations and corporate partners. While the Foundation has successfully engaged local community members as individual donors, its limited capacity and the district's growing financial needs necessitate focusing resources on securing large, transformational gifts. Bailey (2025a) explains, "We must carefully balance our development efforts between cultivating relationships with all supporters while directing our limited resources toward opportunities that can address the significant funding challenges facing our district."

Programs and Impact

As summarized in Box 8.1, the Foundation's programs are organized in four broad areas: Academic Excellence with Purpose, Clear Pathways to Meaningful Futures, Well-being as a Foundation for Success, and Scholarships (Bailey, 2025b). The IPSF is a conduit for grants from outside funders to support school district programs. It cultivates and solicits support consistent with funders' grantmaking programs and then manages and grants those restricted funds to the school district. The IPSF provides financial oversight to ensure that expenditures occur in alignment with donor intentions and grant parameters. As Bailey (2025a) describes the process, "we have many conversations with the superintendent's team to understand the components of programming, identifying the costs and expected outcomes. That goes into a proposal and then we talk with the funder. It's a back and forth process."

The highest priority for the school district at the time that Bailey spoke to the authors in 2025 was support for post-secondary readiness. Funding secured by IPSF supports activities such as students going on college tours, having access to dual credit courses, participating in rigorous coursework associated with specific career pathways, and having experiential learning opportunities outside the classroom. Other priority areas include STEM education, literacy, and teacher professional development (Bailey, 2025b). Given the Foundation's role as an intermediary between private funders and the school district and the restricted nature of most grants, outcome measures generally are agreed upon in advance by the grantmaker and the district. Those measures may include internal or external data, selected to indicate whether the grant has "hit the mark" (Bailey, 2025a).

The Foundation keeps its board and donors informed of trends and developments in education, but in view of its status as a charitable nonprofit and its relationship with the school district, it does not engage in advocacy or lobbying (Bailey, 2025a).

Box 8.1 Indianapolis Public Schools Foundation Strategic Initiatives

Academic Excellence with Purpose

We fund programs that elevate classroom learning through well-prepared teachers and inspiring curriculum that engages students at every level.

Clear Pathways to Meaningful Futures

We support initiatives that prepare students for success beyond graduation, from early career exploration to comprehensive post-secondary readiness. This includes work-based learning experiences, career pathways, dual credit opportunities, and other programs that connect classroom learning to real-world success.

Wellbeing as a Foundation for Success

We invest in comprehensive student wellbeing through mental health resources, social-emotional learning programs, and athletic opportunities. Our approach develops the whole child by supporting mental resilience, healthy relationships, and physical wellness through sports and recreation, ensuring every student has the foundation needed to thrive.

Scholarships

The IPS Scholarship Program is made up of over 13 scholarship funds. There is a specific fund for each IPS High School: Arsenal Tech, Crispus Attucks, George Washington, and Shortridge. Additionally, all IPS seniors are eligible for the General Scholarship Fund. The other scholarship funds have special consideration for certain interest areas including but not limited to art, athletics, music, language arts, STEM, cosmetology, building trade, and more.

SOURCE: Bailey, Stephannie. 2025b. Email to authors May 19, 2025. Used with permission.

Trends and Challenges

Stephannie Bailey observes that the Foundation's model involves connecting funders' interests with district initiatives that requires that the IPSF staff engage in close contact with funders and also remain well-informed about the district's priorities, requiring continuing dialog with the district's leadership. The required communication can be time-consuming for all parties (Bailey, 2025a).

Bailey identifies changing public policy with regard to education as presenting new challenges, both for school districts and public school education foundations. Such changes are sure to have an impact on the role of the foundations. At the time Bailey spoke with the authors, in 2025, legislation under consideration in Indiana intended to reduce property taxes, a primary source of revenue for public schools, and require that districts share property tax revenue with independent charter schools located within their geographic boundaries, but operating outside of district control. Similar legislative initiatives existed in other states as well. In addition, there was uncertainty about the future of federal funding impacting public education.

The full implications of such policy changes could not be fully assessed at the time that Bailey (2025a) spoke, but she observed that in light of reduced public funding, "private philanthropy may become where we need to go to secure funds for public schools." However, the challenge is that private funders may not be interested in providing unrestricted operating support to help the district address shortfalls in appropriated funds. The district may need unrestricted funds to offset declining tax revenue, but IPSF still has to present private funders with specific initiatives. "We might ask for unrestricted funds," Bailey (2025a) explained, "but many funders want to do new things rather than support general operating budgets. The funder wants to see innovation, while the superintendent is trying to keep the doors open in the face of budget cuts."

The case for general operating support may be especially unattractive to some corporate donors, who may suggest the need for greater efficiencies in school operations. However, priorities among corporate funders vary and may be matched against district needs. For example, some favor college readiness programs, while others are interested in teacher development, STEM education, or other areas. Bailey (2025a) predicts that the Foundation will need to continue being "the matchmaker, understanding the district's needs and taking those to the funder that cares about that particular topic."

Bailey serves on the board of directors of the Indiana Association of Public Education Foundations and is also a member of a smaller group of executives of foundations across the country that have similar models, which meets once a month. She observes the wide variation in the size and operation of foundations in various districts in her state and others. Some are led in large part by volunteers and raise funds primarily through events. Others have larger staffs and raise significant amounts. She predicts that in an era of growing financial pressures and constraints, districts without foundations will need to create them and districts that currently have foundations will be looking to them for increased philanthropic support.

Bailey (2025a) notes that having a foundation is of great advantage to public school districts, since, among other benefits, it helps to bring continuity to fundraising efforts and creates a positive relationships with donors. School district leadership may change, but relationships established by the foundation's leadership may help to bridge such transitions, enhancing those relationships and increasing philanthropic support.

References

Bailey, Stephannie. 2025a. Interview with authors, April 14, 2025.

Bailey, Stephannie. 2025b. Email to authors, May 19, 2025.

Indianapolis. 2025. Britannica. Accessed March 24, 2025. https://www.britannica.com/place/Indianapolis-Indiana

IPSF (Indianapolis Public Schools Foundation). 2023. Form 990. Accessed April 8, 2025. https://projects.propublica.org/nonprofits/organizations/311103966/202413199349301681/full

IPS (Indianapolis Public Schools). 2025. District Overview. Accessed March 25, 2025. https://myips.org/about-us/district-overview/

IPSF (Indianapolis Public Schools Foundation). Website. Accessed March 25, 2025. https://www.ipsfund.org/

9 Fund for the School District of Philadelphia

Philadelphia, the largest city in Pennsylvania, has a unique place in the history of the nation. Founded in 1682 by William Penn, it was the location of the signing of the Declaration of Independence and the Constitutional Convention of 1787. Both events occurred in Independence Hall, which houses the Liberty Bell and is now a part of Independence National Historical Park. The city's name translates to "brotherly love" in the Greek language and it is sometimes known as "the City of Brotherly Love," a sentiment that also reflects the Quaker values of its founder. Also commonly called just "Philly," it is both a seaport and an industrial center. Philadelphia has a rich array of cultural institutions and is home to multiple universities, including the University of Pennsylvania, Temple University, and Drexel University (Trussell and Stevens, 2025).

The School District of Philadelphia is an independent district, governed by a board of education appointed by the mayor and confirmed by the city council. The board also authorizes charter schools and appoints the superintendent. At the time of this writing, that position was held by Dr. Tony B. Watlington, Sr., who had served since 2022 (SDP, 2025). The district is the nation's eighth largest, enrolling more than 117,000 students in district-managed and alternative schools and more than 64,000 in charters. The student body is diverse, including 49 percent of students who are Black and 25 percent who are Hispanic/Latino (SDP, 2025). More than 20 percent of students are from backgrounds defined as poverty (DCES, 2023). The district's budget in 2025 was more than $4.5 billion (SDP, 2025).

Fund for the School District of Philadelphia: History and Overview

The Fund for the School District of Philadelphia (FSDP) is an independent 501(c)(3) organization that functions as the official nonprofit arm of the School District of Philadelphia. It serves only the traditional public schools in the district, while the charter schools are responsible for their own fundraising. While there are some other organizations that direct funds to specific purposes in the schools, FSDP is "the only philanthropic organization that works directly with school leadership to align the investments of partners—private foundations, corporations and businesses, community organizations and individual donors—with the strategies that will impact the success of students attending our neighborhood public schools" (FSDP, 2025a).

The Fund celebrated its tenth anniversary in 2025, having raised more than $64 million in the preceding decade (FSDP, 2025b). There was a predecessor organization that was created in 2003, but it functioned exclusively as a fiscal intermediary, receiving grants and distributing the funds to the district, with no active fundraising programs. The superintendent in 2015, Dr. William R. Hite Jr., saw the need for an organization that would proactively raise funds for district priorities, which led to the transformation and rebranding that resulted in the Fund for the School District of Philadelphia as it is today.

Kathryn Epps was appointed as the Fund's president and chief executive officer in 2023, having previously served as the executive director of a nonprofit, the Hire Philly Coalition, where she focused on workforce development. While she had not previously worked in public education, she observes alignment between her previous and current responsibilities, saying "We're all working on the cradle-to-career continuum, just on different segments" (Epps, 2025).

The Fund is focused on fundraising and maintains a staff that includes a vice president of development and other development professionals. Fundraising also accounts for a high portion of the president's time. At the time of Kathryn Epps's conversation with the authors in 2025, plans included the establishment of additional fundraising positions. In addition to its own staff, the Fund engages external consultants and contractors related to marketing and finance.

The FSDP is an independent nonprofit and Epps reports to its board rather than the school district; however, there is a close relationship between the two entities. The Fund is the official fundraising arm of the district, established through a school board resolution and defined in a contract that is renewed every three years. Epps serves as a member of superintendent's cabinet, the only non-district employee to do so. The cabinet meets weekly and, in addition, Epps meets one-on-one with the superintendent and other school officials, remaining "very much in tune with day-to-day workings of the district" (Epps, 2025).

The school district has a strategic plan, titled Accelerate Philly. Being the district's first publicly-available strategic plan, it specifies goals and intended outcomes over the period of 2023–8 in five priority areas: improve safety and well-being; partner with families and communities; accelerate academic achievement; recruit and retain diverse and highly effective teachers and talent; and deliver efficient, high quality, cost-effective operations (FSDP, 2025c). Development of the district's strategic plan was a collaborative process and the intention was for FSDP to be engaged in its development. However, the process occurred at a time when there was a vacancy in the Fund's CEO position; as such the collaboration did not occur. The district's strategic plan was released soon before Epps's arrival and she recognized the need to connect the Fund's work with the priorities it articulated. She decided to do so by defining an initiative called Funding Accelerate Philly, with fundraising objectives tied to the district's priorities. The goal of Funding Accelerate Philly is to secure $40 million over five years to advance goals of the plan. When asked if Funding Accelerate Philly is formally a fundraising campaign, Epps acknowledged that it has characteristic consistent with that concept, including a goal and deadline, although it does not formally carry that label (Epps, 2025).

Governance and Board Role

In 2025, the FSDP was governed by a board of seventeen members, including business executives, educators, and individuals from other fields. The bylaws do not establish term limits and do not include a requirement for board giving or participation in fundraising. Epps (2025) notes that the bylaws have been in place for a long time and have not evolved to include provisions common to many nonprofit organizations now. Speaking in 2025, she reported that a consultant had been hired to review the bylaws and engage in board development activities, with the likelihood that some changes might be forthcoming.

Fundraising and Philanthropy

Of the total revenue of the FSDP, approximately 48 percent is derived from private foundations, 22 percent from corporations and corporate foundations, 10 percent from state and local governments, 5–7 percent from board-based individual giving, 5 percent from major gifts received from high net-worth individuals, and the rest from crowdfunding and events (Epps, 2025). As Kathryn Epps notes, these percentages can be expected to vary from one year to another.

Given the importance of foundation support, a major part of FSDP's fundraising activity is grant writing, that is, the development of proposals in response to foundation priorities. The staff is well versed in the grant cycles of the major foundations in the region and actively monitors available opportunities that align with the school district's needs (Epps, 2025). Corporations in the Philadelphia area also have giving programs with stated priorities, but offer somewhat more flexibility than private foundations. Epps (2025) explains that sometimes creativity is required to identify school district priorities that may be a good fit with the corporation's giving interests and also a continuing effort to build and maintain relationships with corporate leaders.

While focusing on grants and larger gifts, the Fund also has worked to engage a broader base of individual donors. It offers a crowdfunding platform, known as Philly FUNDamentals, used to market school-based campaigns. The platform permits donors to select a specific public school and make a gift to address its particular needs, as identified by that school's leadership (FSDP, 2025d). It also oversees the Philadelphia Public School Giving Circle, members of which can vote on micro-grant proposals, ranging from $250 to $500, submitted by local educators and school staff on a quarterly basis (FSDP, 2025e).

A current strategy is to increase support in the form of major gifts, generally received from high net-worth individual donors. Epps views this as essential to the Fund's growth and its impact on public education. She sees the Fund's current reliance on foundations as a limitation and a risk. The existing pool of philanthropic resources in Philadelphia is inadequate to meet the city's overall needs and some foundations have ceased operations in recent years. However, there is significant individual wealth in the region. While major gifts from individuals have not been a substantial portion of FSDP's revenue in the past, Epps views it as a promising area for growth.

Epps (2025) observes that people of wealth traditionally have established family foundations, which continued over generations and, in some cases, grew into well-known and large private foundations that exist today. However, new generations are taking a somewhat different approach to their philanthropy, which Epps thinks may provide an opportunity for the Fund to make its case for their support. In 2025, the Fund hosted an event intended to increase awareness among a selected group of potential major-gift donors and it is continuing to develop relationships with those individuals.

Epps (2025) emphasizes the need to match donor interests with the school district's priorities, as identified in the Accelerate Philly strategic plan. It identifies five priority areas, mentioned previously, which encompass more than sixty strategic actions, defined as outcomes. Not all of the strategic actions may be attractive to donors. For example, as Epps notes, the goal of increasing efficiency in school district operations is admirable, but it does not provide an obvious gifting opportunity for a private donor. She explains,

> The process involves a healthy balance between understanding the needs of the district while also recognizing that we have an incredible amount of insight into the funding world that the district does not have. That requires matching and aligning our insights on donor interests with where the funding is needed and determining how we can marry those things in the middle. (Epps, 2025)

Grounding fundraising in the district's identified priorities also helps to avoid situations in which a donor might try to influence district's directions according to their own views.

Programs and Impact

The FSDP does not engage in formal advocacy beyond occasional meetings with elected officials. Rather, it seeks to change education through its own fundraising and grants. The Fund's description of its programs and impact were in the process of redefinition when the authors spoke with Kathryn Epps in 2025 and its website was yet to be revised to reflect the most recent vision. In her conversation with the authors, Epps identified the Fund's top-level priorities as *equity*, *innovation*, and *transformation,* as summarized in Box 9.1. These are the "pillars" under which specific programs and initiatives are undertaken.

Box 9.1 Fund for the School Districtof Philadelphia Pillars

- Equity

Assuring that the educational experience is the same for all students across the district.

- Innovation

Testing cutting edge, innovative solutions, technology resources, and other initiatives that increase outcomes and may later be scaled.

- Transformation

Supporting initiatives and programs to bring permanent improvement to the district, including capital projects and efforts that may lead to long-term changes in the education model.

SOURCE: Based on Epps, 2025. Used with permission.

Epps (2025) explains, "Equity means trying to make sure that the educational experience is the same across the board. Visit a sixth grade classroom in Northeast Philadelphia and then drive 45 minutes to Southwest Philadelphia and sit in a sixth grade classroom. That experience should be the same."

As the term implies, innovation includes the piloting of cutting-edge approaches. As Epps (2025) explains, "we are always looking for the latest and greatest resources that we can introduce to students on a small scale. If it works, it can be scaled up." One initiative underway in 2025 was high-dosage math tutoring for students in grades 6–8. Another pilot program, underway in three schools, was titled Power Up. Undertaken in collaboration with the nonprofit organization Big Brothers Big Sisters, this pilot differed from the common after-school mentoring program, since it involved mentors from Big Brothers Big Sisters housed in the school buildings and meeting with students both individually and in groups during school days. Another innovation underway in 2025 was Parent and Family University, involving parents and families in their children's education as well as providing information about educational opportunities that could be available to adults.

The third pillar—transformation—encompasses efforts to bring permanent improvement to the district, its schools, and educational programs. This includes supporting facilities projects, such as libraries, play spaces, and a wellness center, some of which have been addressed through the Fund's crowdfunding platform. It also includes working to achieve permanent changes in the education model.

Epps explains,

> In the K-12 education space, we're very often trying to apply education systems that were designed 50 years ago in today's world, and that just doesn't work. We need to think, operate, and approach things differently now. We've got to rethink what education looks like. It's not just about testing innovations, but really advancing disruptions to the education model. It's not just making sure that every kid has an iPad. It's asking how do we actually apply a new concept of learning and how are we doing it with the student in mind? How do we change the way that we even view education and then make investments that support this new transformative view? (Epps, 2025)

Epps (2025) cites the example of artificial intelligence, which is being more widely embraced in education. She sees some risk but also promise. Epp says,

> Yes, there is the concern that some students might use it to cheat, but the potential is much greater. Tools have been tested now that enable people to see how AI can augment the teaching experience and really streamline some of the tasks, making interactions between student, teacher, parent, and administrator a lot smarter. It really allows the teacher to teach and to be very student-focused, rather than having to spread their time between teaching and grading and administrative work and all of the things that consume the time of someone who has the same 24 hours in a day as the rest of us.

The Fund evaluates the impact of its efforts against the outcomes included in the school district's Accelerate Philly plan, which Epps calls their "north star." In addition, grants from foundations often include outcomes defined by the grantor, which also require measurement and, as mentioned previously, must be matched with the school district's own needs and priorities when seeking funds.

Trends and Challenges

The authors spoke with Kathryn Epps in the spring of 2025. When asked to identify challenges affecting the foundation, she identified uncertainty about the future of federal funding for public education and its impact on Philadelphia in particular. Although FSDP itself does not receive federal funds, the school district receives substantial federal support. Changes in government funding would inevitably affect the Fund's work by impacting the district's needs. Noting that the School District of Philadelphia has been chronically under-funded for many years, she says that reductions "would complicate an already strained system and that would naturally create a more significant need for the types of support that we bring to the table." At the time of her conversation with the authors, Epps was finding uncertainty about federal funding to be a complicating factor in discussions with potential donors. "The most frustrating part of our job right now is not having answers to the questions that people are asking about the future" (Epps, 2025).

Another challenge facing the Fund for the School District of Philadelphia in 2025 was establishing a broader understanding of the nature and scope of its work.

> "Our challenge has been making sure that people truly understand what we do and that they don't have a limited understanding of us based on what we were more than a decade ago. We are trying to make sure that people fully understand the depth and breadth of the work that we do, our value proposition, and that we are not simply a fiscal intermediary. And so, we have been focused on communications and marketing and developing a realistic brand awareness." (Epps, 2025)

When asked to identify trends affecting the future of all public school education foundations, Epps returned to the need for significant transformation in education systems and methods, in view of changing technology and other forces. She notes with regret that the positive impacts of technology are likely to be less in large urban school districts than in independent schools and smaller districts in more affluent areas. She states, "That is where, again, the foundations and private sector and individuals can really get involved—to help keep that disparity at bay" (Epps, 2025).

References

DCES. 2023. Enrollment, poverty, and federal funds for the 120 largest school districts, by enrollment size in 2021: School year 2019–20 and fiscal year 2022. Accessed December 12, 2023. https://nces.ed.gov/programs/digest/d22/tables/dt22_215.30.asp

Epps, Kathryn. 2025. Interview with authors, May 5, 2025.

FSDP (Fund for the School District of Philadelphia). 2025a. About the fund. Accessed May 7, 2025. https://www.thefundsdp.org/about/

FSDP (Fund for the School District of Philadelphia). 2025b. The fund's 10th anniversary celebration & fundraiser. Accessed May 7, 2025. https://www.thefundsdp.org/news/2025/02/the-funds-10th-anniversary-celebration/

FSDP (Fund for the School District of Philadelphia). 2025c. Funding accelerate Philly. Accessed May 7, 2025. https://www.thefundsdp.org/funding-accelerate-philly/

FSDP (Fund for the School District of Philadelphia). 2025d. Philly FUNDamentals. Accessed May 7, 2025. https://www.thefundsdp.org/philly-fundamentals/

FSDP (Fund for the School District of Philadelphia). 2025e. The Philadelphia public school giving circle. Accessed May 7, 2025. https://www.thefundsdp.org/philadelphia-public-school-giving-circle/

SDP (School District of Philadelphia). 2025. Website. Accessed April 21, 2025. https://www.philasd.org/about/

SDP (School District of Philadelphia). 2023. Accelerate Philly. Accessed May 6, 2025. https://www.philasd.org/wp-content/uploads/2023/06/SDP_StrategicPlan_June-1-2023.pdf

Trussell, John B. B. and Stevens, Sylvester K. 2025. Britannica/Philadelphia. Accessed April 21, 2025. https://www.britannica.com/place/Philadelphia

10 Children First Fund: The Chicago Public Schools Foundation

Located on the shore of Lake Michigan and sometimes known by its nickname, the "Windy City," Chicago is the third largest city in the United States, with a population of almost three million. The metropolitan area, often called "Chicagoland," includes almost ten million residents. Incorporated in 1837 on land once controlled by Native American nations, the city rapidly became a major center of transportation and commerce and grew rapidly with the expansion of railroads in the nineteenth century and air travel in the twentieth century. It is known for its architecture; for example, the Willis Tower (formerly Sears Tower) is the second tallest building in the nation. Today's Chicago is a center of industry and commerce, second only to New York as a financial center. The city is also well-known for the arts, sports, and world-class educational institutions, including the University of Chicago and Northwestern University, located in nearby Evanston (Duis and Schallhorn, 2025). It has been the home of many notable individuals, including for example, President Barack Obama and Pope Leo XIV.

Chicago Public Schools (CPS) is the fourth largest school district in the United States. It is led by a chief executive officer, who reports to a board of education. The district enrolls more than 325,000 students in 634 schools, including district-run, charter, contract, and alternative schools. The CPS student body is diverse, including a majority who are Black or Hispanic and a substantial portion who are English-language learners (CPS, 2025). At the time of this writing, the mayor appointed a majority of the school board. However, under legislation passed in 2024, the board would become a fully-elected board in 2027 (Schutz, 2024). At the time of this writing in 2025, a search was underway for a new Superintendent/CEO (CPS, 2025).

Children First Fund History and Overview

The Children First Fund (CFF) was created in 1996 at the initiative of the school district. In its early years, it functioned entirely as a fiscal agent that managed grants on behalf of CPS. Its role expanded to include more active fundraising in 2017–18, at the urging of the CEO of CPS at the time, Janice Jackson. Rebecca Clarkin (2025a) explains, "Since that time, there has been a much more focused effort by the Fund to establish relationships with sources of philanthropy for CPS." While there are some other organizations that support schools in Chicago, CFF is the only one with a direct connection to CPS, serving the entire district in partnership with district leadership. Its principal goal is to improve education and equalize opportunity for students (Clarkin, 2025a). In the fiscal year ending in 2023, the CFF received grants and gifts totaling almost \$14 million and reported expenditures of paid grants of almost \$13 million. The CFF's total assets exceeded \$33 million (CFF Form 990, 2023).

Rebecca Clarkin was appointed as executive director of CFF in January, 2025, following two decades of experience working with youth-serving organizations in Chicago. She served for a decade as an officer at Youth Guidance, as its chief external affairs officer and then as chief operating officer. She led the growth of Youth Guidance from its position as a small Chicago nonprofit to that of an important partner to CPS. Under her leadership, it also expanded to offer programs in eight other cities. She explains, "What I have loved since my first grants manager job has been finding spaces where philanthropy can either fund innovation or support evaluation that proves a new approach. The idea of school partnerships is deeply ingrained in my professional background." (Clarkin, 2025a)

Although an independent 501(c)(3) organization, the CFF has a close relationship with the CPS. The CEO of CPS serves as an ex-officio member of CFF's board. Clarkin is a member of the CEO's cabinet, meeting monthly with the district's leadership. The CFF's fundraising priorities are aligned with the district's five-year strategic plan. At the time of the authors' meeting with Rebecca Clarkin, the Fund did not have its own strategic plan; but Clarkin was anticipating that a planning process would begin in the near future (Clarkin, 2025a).

Governance and Board Role

Under its bylaws, the board of the CFF includes a maximum of thirteen members, who serve without term limits. As mentioned previously, the CEO of CPS serves as an ex-officio member of the CFF board, without a vote. The balance of the board is self-perpetuating and includes members with backgrounds in business, philanthropy, and education. The board includes some foundation officials who have previous experience with the schools and corporate members who are selected to provide a variety of expertise in areas such as law, finance, and communications. Board members from the business community also are selected to facilitate relationships with industries relevant to the Fund's emphasis on college and career access for CPS students and graduates (Clarkin, 2025a). At the time of this writing in 2025, the chair was Alan King, a partner at Riley Safer Holmes & Cancila LLP.

Board members are expected to make a "personally significant" gift, but there is no minimum amount established. Members of the board also are expected to become engaged in fundraising consistent with their ability to help the Fund initiate relationships within their networks, by making what Clarkin (2025a) describes as "warm introductions."

Fundraising and Philanthropy

The CFF has a staff of twelve members, seven of whom have fundraising responsibilities. The executive director is also deeply involved in building relationships with funders. Staff positions include a director of institutional giving, who manages relationships with corporations and foundations, and a director of major gifts, who works with individual donors. Another full-time position is focused on raising funds for programs related to college and career success, including college preparation, career and technical education, STEM schools, and the Chicago Roundup, a cooperative program between CPS and City Colleges of Chicago (CFF, 2025a).

The largest source of philanthropy is foundations, accounting for 78 percent of support, followed by corporations, accounting for 15 percent. The balance of giving comes from individual donors. The Fund's website lists "partners" at various levels above $10,000, including those at $1 million or more, who are members of the Principal's Circle. The site also recognizes donors of gifts-in-kind (CFF, 2025a). Given the importance of foundation support, CFF's fundraising is primarily focused on grant processes and maintaining close relationships with foundation program officers whose areas of focus align with priorities of CPS.

The CFF does not undertake events specifically intended to raise funds, but does organize "convenings" that engage grantmaking partners in substantive discussions related to CPS priorities. As an example, in 2025 the Fund hosted a convening to discuss the CPS' plan for increasing the quality of arts education and providing additional materials for art teachers, under an initiative called "Arts 2.0" (Clarkin, 2025a). Over the course of a year, convenings focus on various CPS priority areas, engaging funders with an interest in those topics. School officials attend the convenings and speak to the district's priorities and initiatives. Following the convening, CFF staff follow up with attendees to discuss specific funding opportunities. As Clarkin (2025a) notes, this model makes efficient use of school officials' limited time while engaging funders in substantive discussions about CPS programs and priorities.

Speaking with the authors in 2025, Clarkin envisioned opportunities for increasing support from various philanthropic sources. While noting that CFF already has close relationships with many corporations, she observes that the business community in Chicago is particularly "robust," including many nationally-prominent companies, which suggests that building additional corporate relationships could be productive. While CFF already has relationships with major private foundations in Chicago, Clarkin sees opportunities for increasing support from family foundations and individuals who have established donor-advised funds (DAFs).

Programs and Impact

The CFF's fundraising priorities align with those of CPS's strategic plan, titled *Success 2029: Together We Rise.* As CFF explains its process,

> we work closely with the CPS community to prioritize philanthropic funding requests that represent the most critical needs and highest-impact opportunities to support CPS students and schools in achieving our strategic goals.... After evaluating the many existing funding opportunities, [we prioritize] initiatives that not only align most directly with District goals, but also adhere to lessons learned from successful philanthropic partnerships of the past. (CFF, 2025b)

As summarized in Box 10.1, CFF's priorities, as of 2025, are within seven categories. Each of the seven categories encompass a variety of programs and initiatives. For example, academic success includes efforts to strengthen the curriculum in key areas, modernize technology, and prepare and support teachers. Donors can choose to become a partner with a specific school or contribute to the Compassion Fund, which provides financial relief and other resources to schools, students, and families. Initiatives related to college access include coaching and campus visits, among other activities. Career-oriented programs include internships and experiential learning opportunities, some guided by industry experts. Chicago Roadmap, a cooperative program involving CPS and City Colleges of Chicago, aims to provide students with a seamless pathway through college and into their careers. Targeted student supports include services to newly-arrived students and to those who face challenging home environments, interventions to address absenteeism, and efforts to re-engage "off-track students," who may be at risk of not completing their education. District programs address student health and wellness through a variety of interventions and provide support to students with disabilities (CFF, 2025b).

At the time of the authors' conversation with Rebecca Clarkin (2025a), two areas of emerging importance included college and career success, and teaching and learning. She anticipated that CFF's strategic planning likely would result in an increased emphasis on direct student impact, a more explicit definition with regard to college and career success, and academic enrichment, a key priority for the funding community.

Box 10.1 Children First Fund

Priority Opportunities for Partnership

Academic Success

- Academic Instructional Core and Enrichment Opportunities

School Partnership

- Compassion Fund to meet urgent needs & reduce chronic absenteeism
- Sponsor-a-School partners companies with a specific school for support

College Access

- College Exposure & Coaching
- Scholarships & Alumni Assistance

Career Connected Learning

- Students Internships & Experiential Learning
- Skilled Trades Exposure

Targeted Student Supports

- Summer and Afterschool Enrichment STEP & Arts

Physical, Mental & Behavioral Health

- Supporting Students with Disabilities
- Comprehensive Student Health & Wellness
- Social-Emotional and Behavioral Interventions

Educator Development

- Teach Chicago
- Developing Exceptional & Diverse Leaders
- Teacher Advisory Council

SOURCE: Clarkin, Rebecca, 2025b. Email to authors, May 22, 2025. Adapted by the authors. Used with permission.

Clarkin (2025a) emphasizes that CFF does not make grants from its own resources, but functions as a connector between the district's priorities and the interests of funders. As she describes, the district might say, "Within the strategic plan priorities, this is what we would like you to emphasize for the coming year." Then there's a conversation in which CFF might say, "We understand the need, but it may not be the highest priority for the philanthropic community. You may want to look at other resources." Or, alternatively, they might state, "Many donors are interested in this, we'll prioritize it as a key goal this year" (Clarkin, 2025a).

The CFF's impact is measured against existing outcomes identified by CPS and incorporated in grants. The CPS website identifies an extensive set of metrics that are used to evaluate programs and school performance (CPS, 2025). As Clarkin (2025a) explains, "There's a process for tracking continuous improvement and using data at CPS, so typically we're formulating outcome measures within specific proposals that are aligned with the metrics that CPS is using already. CFF is then just reporting and stewarding with regard to whatever slice of the project the funder is actually supporting."

Equalizing educational opportunity across CPS is a goal of both the school district and the CFF. The district utilizes an "opportunity index" to map differences across the city and its website provides opportunity index scores for all schools across the district (CPS, 2025). There are funders who wish to have impact in specific underserved neighborhoods and the opportunity index scores can help identify the greatest needs. However, Rebecca Clarkin (2025a) reports that the majority of funders are interested in systemic improvements rather than impact in specific schools or areas. As she observes, those systemic improvements indeed often have "an outsized impact on students who are least well-served by the current state."

Trends and Challenges

When asked to identify challenges faced by the CFF Clarkin noted the atmosphere of "uncertainty" surrounding public education at the time of her conversation with the authors in 2025. That included potential reductions in federal education funding as well as the ending of support related to the COVID-19 pandemic. Filling the gaps will be a challenge for CPS, but Clarkin views the possibility of doing so through philanthropy as likely to be quite limited. She reports, "Philanthropic partners have been really clear with us that they can't possibly fill all of the gaps that are created by federal funding pressures" (2025a).

In observing the larger environment of public school education foundations, Clarkin observes that many are grappling with similar questions, including how to respond to challenges in the broader environment and how to target their efforts for maximum impact. "Because," she concludes, "at the end of the day, that's what all of us are striving to achieve."

References

Clarkin, Rebecca. 2025a. Interview with authors, May 22, 2025.

Clarkin, Rebecca. 2025b. Email to authors, May 22, 2025.

CFF (Children First Fund). 2023. Form 990. Accessed May 24, 2025. https://projects.propublica.org/nonprofits/organizations/364094830/202410939349301906/full

CFF (Children First Fund). 2025a. Website. Accessed May 23, 2025. https://childrenfirstfund.org/

CFF (Children First Fund). 2025b. Partnering for Progress. Accessed May 23, 2025. https://childrenfirstfund.org/partnering-for-progress/

CPS (Chicago Public Schools). 2025. Website. Accessed May 21, 2025. https://www.cps.edu/

Duis, Perry R. and Schallhorn, Cathlyn. 2025. Chicago. Britannica. Accessed May 21, 2025. https://www.britannica.com/place/Chicago

Schutz, Paris. 2024. CPS 101: Inside the leadership crisis, school board shakeup, and upcoming elections. Fox 32 Chicago. Accessed May 21, 2025. https://www.fox32chicago.com/news/cps-101-leadership-crisis-school-board-shakeup-elections

11 Special Education Foundation

St. Louis County is located in eastern Missouri and surrounds the city of St. Louis, although they are separate jurisdictions. St. Louis was established as an independent city in 1876. It provides its own city and county services (City of St. Louis, 2025).

The Special School District of St. Louis County (SSD) was created in 1957, when voters approved a county-wide local school district specifically intended to serve children with disabilities on a county-wide basis. The same referendum established a county-wide tax, specifically dedicated to supporting the new district's programs (SSD, 2025). SSD provides services spanning twenty-two public school districts operating in St. Louis County and is controlled by a governing council and a board of education. The governing council includes representatives from each of the partner districts in the county and appoints the board of education, which provides direct governance of SSD (SSD, n.d.). The board of education appoints the superintendent of schools, who, at the time of this writing, was Dr. Michael Maclin, having held the position since 2024.

The SSD provides programs for students with disabilities across the county and also operates its own schools for those with significant disabilities. As the SSD 2022–7 strategic plan explains,

> SSD provides special education services … to students age three through [twenty-one] in a variety of placements, which are governed by the federal Individuals with Disabilities Education Act (IDEA). Services are based entirely on a student's Individualized Education Program (IEP). Placements range from SSD teachers providing special education services in the student's home school and district (partner district) to students attending an SSD special education school or a private separate

agency. Ninety-seven percent of students receiving SSD services attend school in the school district where they live" (SSD, n.d.).

The SSD also operates career and technical high schools focusing on a variety of professions.

Tim Eby, executive director of the Special Education Foundation (SEF) that serves the district, notes that SSD's model provides benefits for both efficiency and equity. He explains, "There are some very affluent school districts in St. Louis County, and some very poor school districts in St. Louis County. Having a single entity providing special education services across the county provides more equity than you would probably see if each district had to provide its own special education services" (Eby, 2025).

Special Education Foundation: History and Overview

The SEF was created in 1984 at the initiative of parents, school district staff, and elected officials who recognized the need to supplement public funds with private resources to support special education programs offered by SSD. It was the first education foundation created in Missouri, although some school districts now have their own affiliated foundations. The SEF was a volunteer-run organization until 2003, when the first executive director was appointed, initially on a part-time basis.

Tim Eby was appointed as the full-time executive director of SEF in 2022. He previously led nonprofit public radio organizations in three cities. Before joining SEF, he was the director and general manager of St. Louis Public Radio from 2009 until 2020. He also served on several local and national nonprofit boards, including Easter Seals Midwest, Focus St. Louis, and National Public Radio. He is a board member of the National Association of Education Foundations and the St. Louis Civic Pride Foundation. Eby explains that he has family members who are on the autism spectrum and his personal experience made the position especially attractive to him.

Since accepting the position of executive director, Eby has worked to streamline the Foundation's operations. These efforts haveincluded introducing a CRM system and updated accounting software as well as building a modest-sized staff. As of 2025, the Foundation has a staff of three, including the executive director, a communications and program manager, and an events manager. In addition, SEF engages contractors for grantwriting and management of its annual golf tournament, a major source of funding. Another contractor is engaged to manage the Foundation's high school leadership program, which is discussed further in a subsequent section of this case study.

The SEF is an independent 501(c)(3) organization. It is housed in its own facilities and Eby is employed by the Foundation rather than the district. However, SEF enjoys a positive relationship with the Special Education District. The superintendent of schools attends foundation board meetings and Eby attends school board meetings and reports on the Foundation's work.

At the time of his conversation with the authors, Eby was working to formalize a memorandum of understanding between SEF and SED, which he thought would bring greater clarity to the relationship (Eby, 2025). In his view, the Foundation's work might benefit from enhanced visibility, perhaps resulting from a closer partnership with the district's communications programs. As he explains, "Teachers and families who benefit from our programs love us, but our organization could be better known, both among staff in the district as well as parents. I think telling the story of the things we're doing to impact students' lives also can reflect well on the school district" (Eby, 2025).

Tim Eby notes that some public school foundations are more closely integrated with the districts they support and that SEF's independence has both advantages and disadvantages. Among the disadvantages of independence is the inability to access student records, including contact information that might be useful for informing families about the Foundation's programs, among other purposes. The barrier is particularly substantial given the district's focus on special education. As Eby explains, the records of special education students include their Individualized Education Program, which is based on medical information that is strongly protected by privacy laws and regulations.

Governance and Board Role

The Special Education Foundation is governed by a board that included seventeen members at the time of this writing. The bylaws were revised during Eby's time as executive director to provide for up to twenty-four members and to include term limits, permitting members to serve up to three terms of three-years each. The board includes individuals from local businesses, community citizens, and former school officials. Currently, there are no school officials serving on the board. Eby (2025) observes that most board members have a personal connection "either to an educator or a person with a disability." He views that connection as important because "one of the foremost qualities for any board member is to have a passion for the organization's mission."

The board include an executive committee, a program committee, a finance committee, a governance committee, and a development and marketing committee. It has a give-or-get policy, requiring that board members contribute or raise a minimum of $1,000. Tim Eby notes that the minimum is not a "high bar" compared to some other boards, but it permits every member to participate and, indeed, many board members give more than the minimum.

Fundraising and Philanthropy

The SEF receives its largest portion of revenue from fundraising events, notably from its golf tournament, which raised $340,000 in the fall of 2024. Support for the tournament comes from individuals and corporate sponsors, some of whom are school-district vendors. The tournament and other events combined account for about 60 percent of the Foundation's total revenue. The second largest source is grants from private foundations, which account for about 26 percent, with the balance from individual gifts. Sources of individual gifts include voluntary payroll deductions from school district staff and the Foundation's participation in Giving Tuesday and Give STL Day, a local crowdfunding initiative.

Tim Eby identifies increasing individual support as a high priority, noting that individuals are the largest source of philanthropy nationally. However, he recognizes some challenges in this area. Other public school education foundations associated with districts in St. Louis County also have foundations and have had success in raising funds from individuals, including alumni. However, since SSD alumni are those who have participated in special education programs, many have disabilities that may affect their financial status. In addition, as mentioned previously, privacy requirements limit the Foundation's ability to access contact information.

Programs and Impact

The Special Education Foundation's programs, summarized in Box 11.1, include support for school district programs, assistance to students and families, and a leadership program that the Foundation manages directly.

Box 11.1 Special Education Foundation Programs

We aim to empower students with disabilities by giving them the tools they need to succeed.

Adaptive & Assistive Equipment
The Adaptive Equipment program provides augmentative communication devices and assistive equipment, as well as hearing aids and eyeglasses to students with impairments to help them become more independent.

Arts in the Classroom
Bringing arts and music programs to schools to enhance self-esteem, increased social interaction, improved language skills, and a greater awareness of the arts.

Autism Independence Project
Helping students improve independence by increasing social skills and expanding their meaningful life aspirations.

Classroom Innovation Grants
Classroom Innovation Grants fund innovative projects conceived by Special School District (SSD) educators to help students with disabilities enrich learning and social interactions.

Critical Needs
By providing basic day-to-day supplies, the Critical Needs program provides immediate financial assistance to students to secure essential daily needs so they can meaningfully engage in their education.

Fred Saigh Leadership Academy
The Fred Saigh Leadership Academy exposes high-school students with disabilities to local leaders and institutions, teaching them the importance of being involved in the community.

Kid-to-Camp

Camp programs help to maintain educational and social skills momentum for students with disabilities during academic breaks. We cover tuition for eligible students.

Scholarships

John Cary Scholarships recognize college-bound seniors with disabilities who have excelled in school while displaying resiliency, courage and determination.

SOURCE: Special Education Foundation. 2025. What we do. Accessed May 5, 2025. https://sef-stl.org/what-we-do/ Used with permission.

The Foundation's largest grant program provides classroom innovation grants, enabling teachers to fund innovative projects for their students. Teachers apply for grants with proposals that explain how projects are innovative, may be replicable, and require funding beyond what public funds provide. The grants are based on those criteria.

As an example of a classroom program that he views as especially effective, Eby cites an initiative that involved taking a fourth grade class at one SSD school, where students were severely disabled, to spend a day with students at a private school. He explains that "the inclusive nature of having those students coming together for that experience is highly beneficial. They're having contact with students they may otherwise never meet."

Although classroom grants are not based on student financial status, other programs do take need into consideration. As Eby (2025) explains, "One of the goals that we focus on more than anything else is having positive impact for students who are in places that have the most need." Among students served by the Special School District, 71 percent qualify for free or reduced-cost school lunches, indicating their financial status. Most programs have a financial requirement and families are required to submit tax forms to demonstrate eligibility for such assistance as post-secondary scholarships, summer-camp support, and adaptive equipment, including hearing aids. Among SEF's twenty-two partner school districts, nine are classified as "tier 3," defined by high financial need among students and families. The Foundation focuses its outreach on those areas (Eby, 2025).

The only program directly managed by SEF is the Fred Saigh Leadership Academy. Launched in 2004, the academy offers up to twenty students with disabilities opportunities to explore experiences outside of the classroom that expose them to community leaders and institutions. "They are given the tools and confidence to campaign for school offices, manage significant school projects, and assume leadership positions that they may have previously viewed as beyond their reach" (SEF, 2025). Participation in the academy's programs is not based on financial need, although, as Tim Eby (2025) describes, "we do work very hard to try to get a diversity of students in that mix, because we feel it benefits the experience for students to meet other students from places across St. Louis County that they may not usually encounter."

The Foundation evaluates the effectiveness of all of its programs. In some cases, grants received from private foundations specify outcomes that the grantor expects to be measured. In other cases, SEF undertakes its own evaluation. For example, it requests a report from the teachers who have received classroom grants. It also seeks feedback from both students and parents with regard to its leadership program, college scholarships, and summer-camp assistance. As Tim Eby (2025) explains, "The board's program committee sets goals for all of our programs and has been especially focused on the question of whether we are serving more students." For example, a new program, as of 2025, involves a partnership with iSocial, a company that provides programs for neurodiverse individuals. Called the Autism Independence Program, this initiative focuses on social skills for students with autism and requires payment of a fee, which the Foundation subsidizes for those with need. The Foundation's principal measures are the number of students served and determining that students are receiving adequate support.

The Foundation itself does not engage in formal advocacy, but Tim Eby expresses his own strong views in favor of public education. He states, "Public education is vital to American society and democracy" (Eby, 2025).

Trends and Challenges

When asked to identify the biggest challenge faced by the SEF, Tim Eby (2025) provides a straightforward answer, "Finding the financial resources to achieve the scale necessary to meeting the aspirations we have." The competition for philanthropic support in the St. Louis area is intense. As Eby notes, there are more than 20,000 nonprofits in the region and the number of proposals received by grantmaking foundations is "astronomical." Foundations affiliated with individual school districts in the county raise funds; and the growth of charter schools, which engage in their own fundraising, also increases the competition for education-related philanthropy.

The competition for private foundation grants suggests that SEF needs to increase giving by individuals. As mentioned previously, that will requires overcoming particular challenges faced by SEF. As Eby observes, "In traditional school districts, there are five-year reunions where students want to go back. That just does not happen in the world that we are in here, and so that connection to alumni is just non-existent. I'm not saying that's bad, but it's just different for us." Eby identifies the need for more visibility as essential to increasing support from individuals, saying, "I think the biggest challenge we have is finding our place in the community in order to raise the money necessary to fulfill our aspirations."

Despite challenges, Eby also envisions opportunities and a potentially wider role for SEF. Observing that most school districts have special education students, he is considering how the SEF might share its insights with foundations specifically serving those districts. He also identifies the importance of developing more partnerships, saying "I've always been a believer that we need to find the parade and be a part of the parade, as opposed to trying to create our own. You can get a whole lot farther by working with others to get things done." Among other possibilities, he envisions opportunities to work with employers to hire neurodiverse people, who are often highly effective in many fields. "I think employers see the potential of this workforce, which could really solve a lot of problems for them, but there are often barriers. For example, when a neurodiverse candidate goes through job interviews and doesn't make eye contact, they are often just written off" (Eby, 2025).

At the time of his conversation with the authors in 2025, Tim Eby served as a member of the board of the National Association of Education Foundations, which informed his response to a question regarding the future of such foundations across the nation. Citing potential reductions in public support for education, he sees the role of education foundations expanding, in order to fill the gaps. He observes that many are still primarily volunteer-run organizations and sees the need to increase professionalization across the field, including the development and adoption of best practices. "I think public school foundations can help overcome some of the barriers and challenges that public schools have, working much more closely in partnership with public education in the future. They can help drive improvement and student achievement much higher."

References

City of St. Louis. 2025. City government structure. Accessed May 21, 2025. https://www.stlouis-mo.gov/government/about/city-government-structure.cfm

Eby, Tim. 2025. Interview with authors. May 29, 2025.

SEF (Special Education Foundation). 2025. Fred Saige Leadership Academy. Accessed May 29, 2025. https://sef-stl.org/what-we-do/fred-saigh-leadership-academy.html

SSD (Special School District of St. Louis County). 2025. Website. Accessed May 21, 2025. https://www.ssdmo.org/our-story

SSD (Special School District of St. Louis County). n.d. Specialized for success: 2022–2027 strategic plan. Accessed May 21, 2025. https://resources.finalsite.net/images/v1716575881/ssdmoorg/ld8mv7npxg0y3nbjjefg/2022-27StrategicPlan_2024update012524.pdf

12 Advancing Opportunity, Excellence, and Innovation

This concluding chapter provides a summary and discussion of key points from the case studies included in Chapters 2–11 and some suggestions for those who are working to increase the impact of public school education foundations. As discussed in Chapter 1, readers should bear in mind that the ten foundations discussed in this book are a small sample of public school foundation across the country. They do not represent a random sample and are all associated with medium-to-large urban areas. There are insights to be drawn from these cases, but they may not reflect models that can be adopted by other foundations serving different communities. Indeed, they are different from each other in important ways, reflecting the complexity of public education across the nation and considering the various economic, social, and political variables that impact school districts.

Size and Service Areas

The foundations discussed in this book vary in financial resources, staffing, areas of service, and in other ways. Table 12.1 provides a comparison of revenues, expenditures, and net assets of the foundations obtained from the most recent Form 990s available at the time of this writing. It is important to recognize that this data represents a snapshot at the end of the foundation's fiscal year and revenues and expenditures may vary annually depending on gifts and grants received and awarded. Given this book's focus on how well-targeted expenses through public school education foundations can provide a margin for excellence, Table 12.1 only provides data that indicate the size and scale of foundation activities and not ratios, such as per-student resources,

Table 12.1 Revenues, Expenditures, and Net Assets from Form 990

Foundation/fund (Fiscal year ending)	Total Revenue	Total Expenses	Net Assets
Austin Ed Fund (2023)	$3,302,117	$3,831,266	$4,026,803
Children First Fund: The Chicago Public Schools Foundation (2024)	$17,147,986	$21,889,955	$27,223,403
Denver Public Schools Foundation (2024)	$7,796,710	$9,184,879	$10,947,563
DC Public Education Fund (2023)	$15,409,549	$12,957,784	$19,679,672
Fund for the School District of Philadelphia (2023)	$4,471,465	$5,577,924	$8,508,049
Greater Los Angeles Education Foundation (2023)	$2,695,202	$2,223,005	$4,892,370
Indianapolis Public Schools Foundation (2024)	$5,497,159	$5,470,839	$9,007,488
Jacksonville Public Education Fund (2023)	$2,363,178	$2,485,217	$3,800,750
Knox Education Foundation (2023)	$5,911, 295	$4,917,517	$6,890,971
Special Education Foundation (St. Louis County) (2024)	$492,483	$644,459	$590,373

SOURCE: ProPublica. Nonprofit Explorer. Accessed June 7, 2025. https://projects.propublica.org/nonprofits/

that some previous authors have adopted as measures of effectiveness. As explained in Chapter 1, this study has focused on the foundations' programs and initiatives with the view that even relatively modest but well-targeted investments may provide a "margin" that represents a significant contribution. All of the studies in this volume include interviews with foundation executives. This provides important insights on the impact of foundations that ratios may not reveal.

All of the foundations are professionalized, having chief executive officers and staff positions ranging from three to fifteen, with a median staff size of eight. Many also engage contractors for certain tasks, including proposal-writing, information systems management, and outcome evaluation. The responsibilities of staff positions reflect the focus of the foundation. For example, those that are primarily intermediaries between school districts and grantors engage staff primarily in the areas of proposal-writing and grants management. Those that are pro-active in fundraising from varied philanthropic sources, including corporate and individual donors, employ staff in relevant fundraising positions, some including a vice president or director of development.

Although all but one of the foundations support a single school district, those covered in this book are distinct in other ways. The school districts in Knox County, Duval County, and Denver County are defined on a county-wide basis, encompassing the cities of Knoxville, Jacksonville, and Denver, respectively. School districts in the District of Columbia, Austin, Indianapolis, Philadelphia, and Chicago serve a school district contiguous with a city. The Greater Los Angeles Education Foundation (GLAEF) is unique among the cases considered here, since it serves an entire county, encompassing multiple school districts. It is the philanthropic arm of the Los Angeles County Office of Education and works with eighty districts within the county, many of which have their own affiliated foundations. As CEO Kerry Franco describes, "We fill the gaps for districts that do not have active foundations and support the foundations that are active" (Franco, 2025). The Special Education Foundation, in St. Louis County, Missouri, also is unique among the cases in this book. It serves a single school district and partners with other districts in St. Louis County. The district it serves, the Special School District of St. Louis County, is defined on a countywide basis with the mission of serving students with special needs across multiple other school districts within the county and also with operating some of its own schools. As discussed in the case studies, the foundations also vary in the types of schools they serve, with some limited to traditional public schools and others also supporting charter schools.

Origins and Histories

The ten foundations discussed in this book have varied histories. Some trace their roots to earlier organizations that had limited roles and evolved into the more comprehensive organizations that exist today. For example, the Knox

Education Foundation was created in 2020 through the merger of two pre-existing foundations. Tracing its history to an earlier organization founded in the 1980s, the Jacksonville Public Education Fund was established in 2009. Likewise, the Fund for the School District of Philadelphia was established in 2015, tracing its history to a predecessor organization founded in 2003. The Greater Los Angeles Education Foundation was created in 2019 as an outgrowth of a supporting organization named Friends of LACOE (Los Angeles County Office of Education).

All of the foundations have evolved in their roles and have expanded their missions and activities over any predecessors that may have existed. Some were fiscal agents or made targeted grants before taking on more comprehensive roles. For example, the Denver Public Schools Foundation was established in 1992 and in its early years focused on classroom grants. Its mission broadened to encompass support for district-wide priorities in the 2000s. The Austin Ed Fund was established as the Austin Public Education Foundation in 1993 and has experienced distinct periods in its history. In earlier years it functioned exclusively as a fiscal agent, providing a vehicle for donors to support projects within the school system. It subsequently became the proactive fundraising organization that it is today. The Children First Fund serving the Chicago Public Schools had a similar history, having been established in 1996 and expanding to include more active fundraising in 2017–18. It also should be noted that there are other nonprofit organizations that support public schools in some of the districts, for example by granting scholarships, but the foundations considered in this book are identified as the primary nonprofit partners of their districts.

The impetus for creation of the foundations, or the transformation of their roles, came from varied sources, including groups of private citizens, business leaders, and public officials. In the majority of the cases discussed in this book, the impetus for creating or expanding the foundation came from the school district, with superintendents often playing a leadership role. The DC Ed Fund was founded at the urging of then school chancellor Michelle Rhee, who served from 2007 to 2010 and had a background in philanthropy. The initiative to expand the Denver Public Schools Foundation came from the then-superintendent, Michael Bennet, who is now a United States Senator. The transformation and rebranding that created the Fund for the School District of Philadelphia as an organization that would proactively raise funds for district priorities was undertaken in

2015 under the leadership of then-superintendent, Dr. William R. Hite Jr. The Indianapolis Public Schools Foundation was founded in the 1980s, but later became professionalized at the urging of the school superintendent. The Children First Fund was established in 1996 at the urging of the Chicago Public Schools. And the Greater Los Angeles Education Foundation was created in 2019 at the initiative of the LA County Superintendent of Schools, Dr. Debra Duardo.

Relationship to School Districts and Officials

All ten foundations have close relationships with their school districts and district leadership. While all of the foundations are legally independent 501(c) (3) organizations, some are significantly integrated with their school districts, functioning as the nonprofit arm of the district. All of the foundation chief executives who were interviewed, reported that they meet frequently with school district officials and some serve as a member of the superintendent's cabinet. Some foundations are housed in school facilities, some with a lease agreement or a memorandum of understanding that defines arrangements for the sharing of resources and costs. The Fund for the School District of Philadelphia is identified as the fundraising arm of the district in a school board resolution, defined as a contract that is periodically renewed. In some cases, the foundation staff overlaps with that of the district. For example, the executive director of the Austin Ed Fund also serves as executive director of the district's Office of Innovation and Development (OID), reporting to the superintendent, and the Fund is staffed by OID employees.

Some of the foundation executives who were interviewed identified advantages and disadvantages of their current arrangements and relationships to the school district. For example, being located in school district facilities and having frequent contact with district officials helps the foundation remain well-informed of district priorities, which are the focus of its fundraising efforts. Greater independence provides more flexibility in governance, management, and program development. However, as some of the foundations' CEOs noted, independence also limits access to school district records, including private student data. This may complicate efforts to evaluate the impact of grants and obtain names of parents and alumni for fundraising purposes.

Governance and Board Role

The governing board of a nonprofit organization holds fiduciary responsibility for all aspects of the organization's operations. Some boards are self-perpetuating, with the board electing its own members. In other instances, board members are appointed by an outside authority. Other board members may hold their appointment by virtue of another position, a status defined as ex-officio. Ex-officio members may serve with or without a vote. The organization's CEO often serves as an ex-officio member of the board. It is not unusual to identify hybrid boards that reflect all three methods, including some self-perpetuating, some appointed, and some ex-officio members. The composition of a board may reflect the nonprofit's relationship with another entity, which may appoint board members and/or whose officials may serve in an ex-officio capacity.

In the case of public school education foundations, the composition of the governing board may be revealing of the foundation's relationship to the school district it serves, its sources of support, and other characteristics. For example, foundations that are primarily conduits for grants that support district priorities may find that having school officials serving on their boards is helpful to aligning their efforts with district priorities. Some public school education foundations receive support from government units. Having public officials on their boards may be important to those relationships. Foundations that are engaged in fundraising from corporate and individual donors may design boards that include business leaders and individuals with connections to philanthropy in the community. Some may find that having board members with experience in education is helpful in evaluating the impact of the foundation's initiatives.

Table 12.2 provides a summary of the composition of the governing boards of the ten foundations discussed in this book, at the time of this writing. Three foundations—the DC Ed Fund, the Fund for the School District of Philadelphia, and the Special Education Foundation have no school district or public officials serving on their boards. In contrast, the Knox Education Foundation's (KEF) board of sixteen includes five members who are public or school officials, including the Knox County Mayor, the Knoxville City Mayor, the Chair of the Knox County Commission, the Chair of the Board of Education, and the Superintendent of Schools. As KEF's chief executive officer Mike Taylor explained in his 2025 discussion with the authors, this is an unusual model, which reflects the role of the school district and county in

Table 12.2 Foundation Board Composition

Foundation/Fund	Board Composition*
Austin Ed Fund	The board includes twenty-nine members. The superintendent and the chair of the district's board of trustees serve as ex-officio members, with a vote. Other board members include leaders drawn from businesses and nonprofit organizations in Austin.
Children First Fund: The Chicago Public Schools Foundation	The board includes seven members (maximum of thirteen). The CEO of Chicago Public Schools serves as an ex-officio member, without a vote. The balance of the board is self-perpetuating and includes members with backgrounds in business, philanthropy, and education.
Denver Public Schools Foundation	The board includes twenty-five members. The foundation's CEO, the superintendent of schools, and the chair of the school board serve as ex-officio members. Others include corporate and nonprofit executives and a university official.
DC Public Education Fund	The board is self-perpetuating and includes eight individuals. There are no members who are school officials or who hold ex-officio appointments.
Fund for the School District of Philadelphia	The board has seventeen members, including business executives, educators, and individuals from other fields.
Greater Los Angeles Education Foundation	The board has nine members, including the county superintendent of schools and members of the superintendent's staff, who serve ex-officio with a vote. Other members include community and business leaders.
Indianapolis Public Schools Foundation	The board has nine members. The superintendent and the Board of School Commissioners each appoint one member to the foundation's board. The appointed members serve with a "voice" rather than a vote.
Jacksonville Public Education Fund	The board has eighteen members. The superintendent and the chair of the school board serve as ex-officio members, without a vote, as does the Teacher of the Year.
Knox Education Foundation	The board has sixteen members. The bylaws provide automatic appointments for five, including the Knox County Mayor, Knoxville City Mayor, Chair of the Knox County Commission, Chair of the Board of Education, and the Superintendent of Schools.
Special Education Foundation (St. Louis County)	The board has seventeen members, including individuals from local businesses, community citizens, and former school officials. There are no current school officials serving on the board.

*At time of the authors's conducting the interviews with foundation executives. Data based on information reported by the foundation executives and on foundation websites. Some bylaws provide for a minimum and maximum number of members, so the total membership may vary. Bylaws may be revised from time to time.

creating the foundation and historical funding patterns. Knoxville City, Knox County and Knox County Schools all provided funding to the foundation until 2023. As of 2025, only the Knox County government provided funding to the foundation (Taylor, 2025). Taylor also noted some advantages and disadvantages to this model. As a positive, it enables the foundation board to be a useful forum for discussing priorities and strategies that involve various public entities. As a disadvantage, it creates turnover on the board as terms of public officials automatically expire (Taylor, 2025).

Important governing practices are discussed in the individual case studies, including term lengths, term limits, and committees defined in the bylaws. Boards of organizations engaged in fundraising often have policies regarding board members' philanthropic giving and participation in fundraising activities. The cases in this book provide examples of common variations. Three foundations have no formal policy on board giving or fundraising, although some of those generally encourage such activities. Four foundations have a give-or-get policy, requiring that board members either make personal gifts or secure funding from other sources. Some of those specify a minimum amount. Three foundations have an expectation that board members give an amount proportional to their ability, without stating a minimum amount. Some foundation executives who were interviewed, identified pros and cons associated with each of these approaches.

Fundraising and Philanthropy

Grants from private foundations account for 50 percent or more of revenue at five of the ten public school foundations discussed in this book, and a significant portion for others. One foundation receives 90 percent of its revenue from grantmaking foundations. Corporations are the second largest source of support for several of the public school education foundations studied in this book. Government grants, gifts from individual donors, and revenue from events account for lower percentages.

Some foundation executives who were interviewed, explained that there are private foundations, both local and national in scope that have education as a priority in their grantmaking. They view public school education foundations as partners through which they can pursue their priorities and achieve the desired impact. In working with those grantmaking foundations, staff of school foundations function as intermediaries, matching school district priorities with those of the private foundations, sometimes requiring a time-consuming effort to stay well-informed about the interests on both sides of the potential relationship. As a CEO explained, the school foundation staff is well-versed in the grant cycles of the major foundations and actively monitors available opportunities that align with the school district's needs. As another described, the school foundation's fundraising also requires maintaining ongoing relationships and dialog with grantmaking foundation program officers whose areas of focus align with priorities of the school district. One CEO described the school foundation's approach to private foundation grantmaking as having evolved, saying "In the past, we have been primarily oriented toward responding to RFPs, which of course reflect the priorities of funders. We are now more proactive and focused on raising funds specifically to address school district priorities" (Wallis, 2025).

Corporations are the second largest source of revenue collectively for many of the foundations included in this study, with individual donors generally providing a much smaller percentage of revenue overall. As a foundation's CEO noted, some corporations have established giving programs with stated priorities, similar to grantmaking foundations, but others offer somewhat greater flexibility in responding to school district needs (Epps, 2025). Increasing corporate support is an objective for most of the foundations included in this study, requiring the development of relationships with corporate executives, including as members of the foundation board.

Individual donors are the largest source of philanthropy in the nonprofit sector overall, but comprise a relatively small percentage of revenue for the public school education foundations in this study. Many of the foundations are working to increase support from individual donors. Some are seeking to develop a broad base of individual support, using a variety of methods. Some use traditional methods such as direct mail and email campaigns, and others hold fundraising events. For example, one foundation conducts an annual golf tournament and another an annual telethon in collaboration with a local broadcaster. Others participate in crowdfunding campaigns such as Giving Tuesday and similar local efforts. The Fund for the School District of Philadelphia offers a crowdfunding platform, Philly FUNDamentals, to market school-based campaigns and oversees the Philadelphia Public School Giving Circle. Some recognize donors as members of giving societies defined by their levels of support and provide a listing on the foundation's website.

While many foundation executives mentioned a desire to build a broad base of individual support, one cautioned that the foundation's limited staff resources require remaining focused on sources of larger gifts and grants from foundations, corporations, and a selected number of major gift donors (Bailey, 2025). Others noted obstacles to securing gifts from individual donors, including challenges to securing access to information concerning parents and school district alumni and competition from other nonprofit organizations in their communities.

Some expressed optimism about the potential for securing more major gifts from individual donors. For example, Kathryn Epps (2025) observes that people of wealth traditionally have established family foundations, but new generations are taking a somewhat different approach. The Fund for the School District of Philadelphia is working to engage such individuals through small events and subsequent individual contacts. One foundation's CEO explicitly identified the rapidly-growing area of planned giving, involving gifts made through various financial instruments and estates, as a strategy for increasing individual philanthropy with the goal of building the foundation's endowment (Hazel, 2025).

Programs and Impact

Programs and initiatives undertaken by public school education foundations, including those discussed in this book, commonly encompass professional development for teachers; college and career preparation; scholarships for students; early-childhood and pre-school programs; enrichment experiences beyond the classroom; after-school programs focused on tutoring and training; funding for facilities projects, including play spaces and libraries; direct support to students and families; efforts to assure equity across the districts; programs to prepare students for the impact of rapidly emerging new technologies; and experimentation with innovative programs having the potential to generate systemic change. The individual case studies in Chapters 2–11 provide comprehensive discussions of the foundations' programs that encompass these and other areas.

While the foundations offer programs and initiatives in a variety of areas, four were emphasized with particular frequency in the authors' conversations with foundation CEOs: increasing reading and math proficiency; enhancing college and career readiness; addressing the needs of students in underserved communities within the district; and preparing students to work with emerging technologies. The following are a few examples that illustrate how some are addressing these priorities. The Knox Education Foundation identifies five focus areas for its programs, including overall third grade reading proficiency, overall middle school math proficiency and preparing students for enrollment in higher education, credentialing programs, or armed services. The DC Public Education Fund identifies the DC Reading Clinic, a program launched in 2018 with startup funding from foundations secured by the Fund, as an example of particular success. At the time of the authors' conversation with CEO Jim Kline, the Fund was focusing its planning for new initiatives in two areas—"reimagining math" and "pathways," a program to help students identify their post-secondary directions (Kline, 2025). The Greater Los Angeles Education Foundation supports initiatives to advance digital equity, including development of AI tools and guidelines for districts as well as the expansion of in-person brick and mortar tech centers for high school students. The Jacksonville Public Education Fund identifies literacy as an area of emphasis, with math capability growing in importance. College and career success is a focus area for the Denver Public Schools Foundation. The Austin Ed Fund has defined three focus areas, including early literacy and college and career readiness. Michelle Wallis (2025) identified math is an area of emerging priority for the Fund in 2025.

A high priority for the Indianapolis Public Schools, supported by the Indianapolis Public Schools Foundation, is college and career preparation, including activities such as students going on college tours and participating in coursework associated with specific career pathways. Other priorities include STEM education ad literacy. One initiative underway in Philadelphia public schools in 2025 was high-dosage math tutoring for students in grades 6–8. The Children First Fund, serving the Chicago Public Schools, is engaged in initiatives related to college access and careers, including coaching and campus visits and career-oriented programs including internships and experiential learning opportunities.

Some foundations are addressing inequities within the districts they serve by focusing on underserved areas. For example, the Knox Education Foundation assisted the school district in developing a plan for Region 5, which encompasses downtown Knoxville and includes many schools facing challenges. Working with multiple school districts across Los Angeles County, with various economic profiles, the Greater Los Angeles Education Foundation works to assure that "no educational community is left behind" (Franco, 2025). Equalizing educational opportunity across Chicago Public Schools is a goal of both the school district and the Children First Fund.

The district utilizes an opportunity index to map differences across the city and its website provides opportunity index scores for all schools. There are funders who wish to have impact in specific underserved neighborhoods and the opportunity index scores can help identify the greatest needs (Clarkin, 2025). Executive Director of the Special Education Foundation, Tim Eby, observes that one benefit of having a special education school district and a foundation that serve special education students across multiple other school districts in St. Louis County may be greater equity. The school districts across the county have varied economic profiles and their programs could vary if those districts needed to fund their own special education initiatives (Eby, 2025). Emphasizing the importance of equity as a focus of the Fund for the School District of Philadelphia, CEO Kathryn Epps explains, "Visit a sixth grade classroom in Northeast Philadelphia and then drive 45 minutes to Southwest Philadelphia and sit in a sixth grade classroom. That experience should be the same" (Epps, 2025).

While most foundation programs seek to have a positive impact on current students, teachers, and programs, some focus on the longer term, including educational innovation and systemic change in education systems. For example, the Knox Education Foundation makes grants to fund pilot approaches that may lead to what Mike Taylor calls "systems change" (Taylor, 2025). The DC Ed Fund defines itself as "DCPS' very own venture fund," supporting innovations with potentially significant long-term impact (DC Public Education Fund, 2025). As CEO Jim Kline describes, "We want something that is heavy on the startup costs and shows a path for sustainability" (Kline, 2025). Kathyrn Epps (2025) describes the role of the Fund for the School District of Philadelphia as going beyond innovation to drive "transformation," saying, "It's not just about testing innovations, but really advancing disruptions to the education model.... It's asking how do we actually apply a new concept of learning and how are we doing it with the student in mind?" One interesting innovation described by Sara Hazel, President and CEO of the Denver Public Schools Foundation goes beyond educational reform to consider the possibility of partnerships between education foundations and private businesses, potentially creating new streams of revenue for foundations and public schools. Focused initially on providing affordable housing for teachers, Hazel (2025) envisions other possibilities, such as exploring options with the school district to utilize vacant school buildings for potential revenue generation, perhaps as a location for nonprofits and small businesses to utilize office space and shared services. It is notable that some public university foundations, to which public school foundations were compared earlier in this book, have indeed expanded their activities beyond traditional fundraising to participate in entrepreneurial partnerships involving their universities and private businesses.

One of the topics explored in interviews with foundations' CEOs were methods used to evaluate the impact of their initiatives. In the case of the public school education foundations that serve primarily as intermediaries between private foundations and school districts, outcome metrics are generally defined by the terms of the grants, assuming they are consistent with those of the school district. In other cases, outcomes are evaluated against broader district priorities. For example, the Children First Fund is guided by the Chicago Public Schools strategic plan, Success 2029: Together We Rise, and the Fund for the School District of Philadelphia evaluates its efforts against the district's plan, Accelerate Philly. The Special Education Foundation is unique among those studied, given its mission of supporting students with disabilities and its requirement of financial qualifications for some of its programs. In view of those characteristics, the Foundation's principal measures are the number of students served and assurance that students are receiving adequate support (Eby, 2025). Some foundations maintain a staff position focused on evaluation, while others engage outside evaluators as needed. For example, the Knox Education Foundation maintains a relationship with the Boyd Center at the University of Tennessee, which assists with collecting and analyzing information.

Most of the foundations discussed in this book do not engage in advocacy. Some engage in what might be characterized as soft advocacy, for example, expressing general support for public education. Sam Gelinas (2025) notes that the Greater Los Angeles Area Education Foundation may occasionally offer recommendations based on research findings and the Knox Education Foundation does occasionally communicate with the public about the school system (Taylor, 2025). The Denver Public Schools Foundation historically has not engaged in advocacy, but its board did publicly support a bond issue on the ballot in 2024 because of its implications for school funding (Hazel, 2025). Among the foundations studied, the Jacksonville Public Education Fund was an exception in this area. As Rachel Fortune (2025b) describes, the Fund did support a "sales tax referendum that passed in 2020 and a property tax referendum that passed in 2022," because of their importance to the funding of education. The Fund maintains an Advocacy Center that tracks relevant legislation, provides advice on how citizens can contact their legislators, and offers educational materials on the legislative process. Its website provides a link enabling citizens to identify and contact their elected state representatives (JPEF, 2025).

Trends and Challenges

Foundation executives who were interviewed by the authors were asked to identify trends and challenges faced by their own foundations and to reflect on the future of public school education foundations generally.

There were some common themes with regard to challenges faced by the particular foundations under discussion. Among the points mentioned were insufficient capacity and the difficulty of attracting and retaining staff. One CEO cited the need to better communicate the foundation's role to the public in an era of new media. Unsurprisingly, most CEOs mentioned the challenge of raising sufficient funds to meet the school district's needs and the foundation's aspirations. Some identified trends in philanthropy that have changed the landscape, including the sunsetting of some grantmaking foundations and a new approach to giving by younger generations. Others described intense competition for philanthropy in their communities.

Some mentioned challenges faced by the education sector broadly, including teacher retention and student performance, with some deficits remaining from the era of the COVID-19 pandemic. One mentioned the decline in student enrollment in some regions. As Sam Gelinas (2025) observed, "Enrollment drives everything … including district finance, district staffing, and district facilities."

Most of the foundation executives noted concerns about funding of public education, with implications for the role of their foundations. The interviews were conducted in the first half of 2025, during a period of significant change and uncertainty regarding federal education policies, including the potential elimination of the Department of Education. Such changes held funding implications for many school districts. Some foundation executives also cited funding challenges in their individual states. School districts in Denver and Philadelphia were described as chronically underfunded. Austin had seen recent reductions in school funding. Legislative proposals under consideration in Indiana was intended to reduce property taxes, a primary source of revenue for public schools (Bailey, 2025). The growth of charter schools and voucher-type programs carried implications for the funding of traditional public schools. In 2025, there were proposals in Indiana that would require districts to share property tax revenue with independent charter schools located within their geographic boundaries (Bailey, 2025).

Some interview participants anticipated that public school education foundations might be called upon to fill growing funding gaps. While they generally expressed their desire to address greater needs with increased funding, some also noted challenges in doing so. As Stephannie Bailey (2025) explained, "Private philanthropy may become where we need to go to secure funds for public schools." However, she also noted that many donors have limited interest in providing unrestricted funds to fill gaps in school district's operating budgets, preferring to support innovative and targeted initiatives. "We might ask for unrestricted funds," she said, "but many funders want to do new things rather than support general operating budgets." Rebecca Clarkin (2025) concurred, saying, "Philanthropic partners have been really clear with us that they can't possibly fill all of the gaps that are created by federal funding pressures."

In addition to the problem of sustaining funding for schools, some foundation executives highlighted a broader debate about public education. Some observed that the politicization of issues surrounding education has complicated discussions with donors. As Kathryn Epps (2005) described, "The most frustrating part of our job right now is not having answers to the questions that people are asking about the future." While expressing his support for charter schools, Jim Kline (2025) stated, "We need to continue to fight for the future of public schools and explain why public education matters—to our democracy, to our workforce, to our mental health, to our students with disabilities, and to our students who don't have other options." Acknowledging the challenges presented by the current public dialog, Rachael Tutwiler Fortune (2025b) expressed the hope that public school education foundations might provide "[a] bridge, working to bring key parties together."

Despite multiple challenges, allof the foundation CEOs expressed the view that public school education foundations can play an important and growing role, anticipating continued growth in existing foundations and the establishment of new foundations in districts where they do not currently exist. A few echoed a point made in the opening chapter of this book, that public school education foundations might follow the path of institutionally-related foundations in public higher education, becoming more impactful and integral to advancement of the institutions they support.

Foundation executives offered specific suggestions to accomplish that growth. Unsurprisingly, those included increasing foundations' capacity and expanding fundraising initiatives, especially with individual donors. Another suggestion was establishing and communicating standards of practice and increasing professionalization of foundation staff through training and certification provided by organizations such as National Association of Education Foundations. Others said that it will become increasingly important for foundations to measure and publicize their results. Some see a need for more collaboration among foundations, perhaps facilitated through state associations. Another potential strategy that was suggested is exploring more collaboration between public school education foundations and other nonprofits interested in schools.

Authors' Observations and Suggestions

It must be emphasized again that the sample of foundations discussed in this book is small, just ten, and is not necessarily representative of the thousands of foundations across the country. Indeed, even the foundations discussed in this book demonstrate considerable diversity in their size, relationship to their school districts, programs, and other qualities. Public education is a complex universe. However, the authors offer some modest observations and cautious suggestions that may be of value to those who are seeking to increase the impact of such foundations.

Chapter 1 of this book reviewed some conclusions of researchers who have studied public school education foundations in the past. As discussed in that chapter, the research findings suggest that the most important variables in the success of a foundation are its longevity, the district's size and location, and community wealth, none of which are within its control (Clogston, 2021). However, other studies have identified characteristics that are controllable, including employment of professional foundation staff, the composition of foundation boards, and the relationship between the foundation and the school district (Clogston, 2021). In Chapter 1, the authors distilled the findings of research as offering some basic points of advice: build a paid staff; enlist a strong board that is representative of the community; align the foundation's fundraising priorities with those of the district; and engage the superintendent in the foundation's activities.

Following completion of the ten case studies included in this book, the authors would reiterate those simple suggestions and add a few more.

It is clear that public school districts across the country face a considerable and growing need for resources to supplement public funding, which is threatened at the federal, state, and local levels. The foundation executives who stated that their organizations are unlikely to raise sufficient philanthropic funds to fill the budget gaps left by declining public support are likely correct. The magnitude of needed funds and the reluctance of private donors to provide unrestricted gifts to support general operating budgets is a reality for most fundraising institutions, including universities. However, the programs and initiatives supported by the foundations discussed in this book are impactful and worthy of greater support. Obtaining that support will require building professionalized fundraising operations and investing more in fundraising initiatives. It also will require collaborative efforts including foundation staff, board members, and public school officials.

Private grantmaking foundations and corporations are likely to remain the principal source of support for public school education foundations in the foreseeable future, but individual donors are by far the largest source of philanthropy in the United States. Efforts to build a broad base of support from individuals are worthwhile, partly because they engage those individuals and help to strengthen their understanding and commitment to public education. Research suggests that people who become donors to an organization often come to identify with it and become its advocates. However, broad-based fundraising is not the most cost-effective strategy for increasing total support. Such activities as events, and online fundraising may engage substantial numbers of individuals and build a pipeline of donors who eventually may provide major gifts. But that can be a long process and the investment of time, effort, and expense must be balanced by that understanding. The reality of fundraising in the current time is that major gifts account for a disproportionate percentage of all individual philanthropy. Indeed, one of the most rapidly-growing components is planned giving, reflecting the aging of the population and the fact that individual net worth tends to increase with age. Expanding efforts to engage and develop relationships with potential major-gift donors would seem as an option that school foundations should consider.

Securing major gifts requires more than asking for them. It requires a process of identifying those with the financial capacity to give significant amounts, advancing substantive relationships with them, and engaging them in the work of the organization for which their gifts are needed. The process can be guided by professional fundraising staff, but also must engage others. This suggests that foundation boards need to be actively involved in the process and that school officials, including superintendents, also must play important roles. It also may be useful for some foundations to explore creating various advisory councils, a strategy that other nonprofits and higher education institutions have found to be an effective strategy for engaging additional individuals in substantive ways.

Another area worthy of exploring involves partnerships between public school education foundations and businesses that go beyond philanthropy. For example, as mentioned previously, the Denver Public Schools Foundation is exploring partnerships to provide more affordable housing for teachers and possibly repurpose abandoned school district real estate to produce commercial revenues. In higher education, some university-related foundations have experienced success with this approach. For example, the Kent State University Hotel and Conference Center is the result of a public-private partnership between The Pizzuti Companies and the Kent State University Foundation. Indeed, while many donors may not provide unrestricted gifts to meet current operating needs, it is possible that commercial partnerships might do so to some extent.

In many cases, public school education foundations compete for support with a variety of nonprofit organizations in their communities and with fundraising for individual schools, including charter schools. Succeeding in that environment requires developing a strong case for support, that is, a rationale for why they are worthy of donors' attention. This case may involve a variation of the "margin for excellence" concept, discussed in Chapter 1, which was successfully employed by public colleges and universities to explain the potential impact of philanthropy at a time when many people did not view those tax-supported institutions as worthy targets of their giving.

We would suggest a variation on the margin-for-excellence case that seems well-suited to the contributions that public school education foundations are making today and which we have captured in the subtitle of this book: *providing a margin for opportunity, excellence, and innovation*. That would encompass the goals of the foundations discussed in this book and others. It explains why their contributions are important and impactful, even if not of sufficient magnitude to provide core operational funding for school districts.

It will be essential to undertake effective communication of that case for support and of results, so that donors can understand the impact of their gifts. Some of the 117 foundations that the authors reviewed before selecting the ten for case studies have robust websites that provide such information. However, many do not. Some provide little information on their programs, sources of support, or impact. And, of course, it will be essential to go beyond websites to utilize social media and other communication platforms.

Increasing the professionalization of foundations will require strengthening collaboration, sharing best practices and data, and training foundation staff. As mentioned earlier in this book, higher education is served by organizations such as the Association of Governing Boards and the Council for Advancement and Support of Education, which address the practices of sound governance and institutional advancement (including fundraising), respectively. Organizations such as the National Association of Education Foundations, and various state associations, may come to play similar roles in public education.

All of the foundations studied in this project are situated in complex environments, having various relationships with the school districts they support and with officials in the school district and other public agencies. While all of the CEOs described having positive relationships with school district leadership, it is important for districts to encourage and facilitate their work and help build understanding of their foundations' importance. As some foundation executives described, school officials face enormous demands on their time, attention, and resources. It may be challenging for them to dedicate more effort to working with their foundations, but the long-run benefit to their districts and to public education may be substantial and worthy of their considerable attention. The foundations may bring resources that lead to significant positive impact on current students, innovations, and transformations that will benefit students now and in the future. In addition, they can be bridges to the private sector and communities, helping to increase understanding and support for public education. In his interview with the authors, Mike Taylor, the then CEO of the Knox Education Foundation and chair of the National Association of Education Foundations, offered an insight on public school education foundations that is worthy as a conclusion to this discussion: "We navigate not just the nonprofit sector, but also the public sector.... Foundations bring in money for schools from the private sector, but they also help the private sector understand the intricacies of public schools, which involve local, state, and national processes that must be navigated to bring change" (2025).

References

Bailey, Stephannie. 2025. Interview with authors, April 14, 2025.

Clarkin, Rebecca. 2025. Interview with authors, May 22, 2025.

Clogston, N. G. 2021. The influence of private contributions in public education: An examination of education foundations. Dissertation, University of Houston-Clear Lake.

DC Public Education Fund. 2025. Website. Accessed January 27, 2025. https://dcedfund.org/

Eby, Tim. 2025. Interview with authors. May 29, 2025.

Epps, Kathryn. 2025. Interview with authors, May 5, 2025.

Fortune, Rachael Tutwiler, 2025b. Email to authors, April 30, 2025.

Franco, Kerry. 2025. Interview with authors. March 7, 2025.

Gelinas, Sam. 2025. Interview with authors. March 7, 2025.

Hazel, Sara. 2025. Interview with authors, May 1, 2025.

JPEF (Jacksonville Public Education Fund). 2025. Advocacy center. Accessed April 23, 2025. https://www.jaxpef.org/advocacy-center/

Kline, Jim. 2025. Interview with authors, February 3, 2025.

Taylor, Mike. 2025. Interview with authors January 23, 2025.

Wallis, Michelle. 2025. Interview with authors, March 28, 2025.

Suggestions for Further Reading

Book Chapter, Articles, and Dissertations

Abzug, R., Olbrecht, A., Sabrin, M., and DeLeon, E. 2016. Nonprofit financing to the rescue? The slightly twisted case of local education foundations in New Jersey. *Nonprofit and Voluntary Sector Quarterly*, 45 (1), pp. 133–149.

Clogston, N. G. 2021. The influence of private contributions in public education: An examination of education foundations. Dissertation, University of Houston-Clear Lake.

Moore, James H., Jr. 2019. Institutionally related foundations in public colleges and universities. In Worth, M. J. & M. T. Lambert, *Advancing higher education: New strategies for fundraising, philanthropy, and engagement*. Rowman & Littlefield, pp. 197–210.

Nelson, A. A. & Gazley, B. 2014. The rise of school-supporting nonprofits. *Education Finance and Policy*, (4), pp. 541–566.

Nisbet, E. 2021. Local-level philanthropic partnerships in public education: Dilemmas for equity and public responsibility. *Journal of Urban Affairs*, 43(2), pp. 251–269.

Websites

Association of Governing Boards of Universities and Colleges (AGB): https://agb.org/

Council for Advancement and Support of Education: https://www.case.org/

National Association of Education Foundations: https://www.educationfoundations.org/

About the Authors

Michael J. Worth

Michael J. Worth is Professor of Nonprofit Management in the Trachtenberg School of Public Policy and Public Administration at the George Washington University. He teaches graduate courses on governing and managing nonprofit organizations, managing fundraising and philanthropy, and related topics. He serves as director of the school's Graduate Certificate in Nonprofit Management program.

He was a public school teacher early in his career and subsequently pursued a career in higher education. He served as Vice President for Development and Alumni Affairs at the George Washington University and previously as Director of Development at the University of Maryland. Earlier in his career, he was Assistant to the President at Wilkes University and Director of Development at DeSales University.

In addition to many articles in academic and professional journals, he has written or edited widely-read books related to fundraising, philanthropy, and higher education. He is the author of two textbooks, Nonprofit Management: Principles and Practice (7th edition, 2024) and Fundraising: Principles and Practice (2nd edition, 2025), which are widely adopted for undergraduate and graduate courses.

He holds a B.A. from Wilkes University, an M.A. in economics from the American University, and a Ph.D. in Higher Education from the University of Maryland.

***

Sanjay K. Pandey

Sanjay K. Pandey is Shapiro Professor of Public Policy and Public Administration in the Trachtenberg School of Public Policy and Public Administration at the George Washington University. Professor Pandey's scholarship focuses on public policy and public administration, and deals with questions central to leading and managing public organizations. Professor Pandey directed two landmark surveys of public organizations (Phase II and Phase IV of the National Administrative Studies Project). Professor Pandey's scholarship has been recognized with numerous awards. Two of his co-authored articles are included among the Public Administration Review's seventy-five most influential articles. This selection includes contributions from eminent scholars including Herbert Simon and Elinor Ostrom.

Professor Pandey was awarded the NASPAA/ASPA Distinguished Research Award in 2013, an award recognizing "substantial impact on public administration." In 2014, Professor Pandey was elected a Fellow of the National Academy of Public Administration. In 2022, he was honored with the H. George Frederickson Award for Career Contributions to Public Management Research. In 2023, Professor Pandey was honored with the Dwight Waldo Award for distinguished career contributions to public administration, and the Herbert Simon Award for distinguished contributions to the scientific study of bureaucracy. An extended version of Professor Pandey's Herbert Simon Lecture titled, "Elevating subjective individual experience in public policy and public administration: Reflections on red tape, administrative burden, and sludge" was published in the *Public Administration Review*. In 2024, Professor Pandey was awarded the Honey W. Nashman Spark a Life for Faculty Member of the Year Award for positive mentoring relationships and impact on holistic development of students.

At George Washington University, Professor Pandey, in collaboration with his colleagues, has convened several academic conferences bringing together leading academic researchers from the United States and abroad. He is co-founder and convener of the Mixed Methods Research Interest Group at the George Washington University.

***

Holly Kamm Wahl

Holly Kamm Wahl, MBA was appointed by the Commissioners as the Town Manager of the Town of Oxford, Maryland, in January 2025. In this capacity, Ms. Wahl provides direct oversight of the town's day-to-day operations, including all governmental functions and services, carrying out legislative actions of the Commissioners. Prior to serving as the town manager of Oxford, Ms. Wahl served as the town administrator for the Town of Chesapeake Beach, MD and held the positions as director of operations for a general contractor, the director of operations for a 24/7 homeless shelter and homeless support center, and the chief operating officer for a government contractor.

Ms. Wahl holds a Bachelor of Science degree in Business Administration from the Johns Hopkins University, a Masters in Business Administration (MBA) from the University of Maryland, and has obtained executive certificates in Public Administration & Public Policy from the Harvard Kennedy School and the University of Maryland. As of 2025, Ms. Wahl was in the final dissertation phase of obtaining her Doctorate in Public Administration & Public Policy at the George Washington University. Ms. Wahl is credentialed manager of the International City Managers Association (ICMA) and was inducted into the Pi Alpha Alpha Global Honor Society for Public Affairs and Administration George Washington University Chapter in April 2024. Pi Alpha Alpha is an internationally recognized honor society that recognizes outstanding scholarship and accomplishment in public affairs and administration.

www.ingramcontent.com/pod-product-compliance
Ingram Content Group UK Ltd.
Pitfield, Milton Keynes, MK11 3LW, UK
UKHW020648110926
475431UK00001B/50

9 798765 188514